GOD WEARS HIS OWN WATCH

Glimpses of God
& Answered Prayer
at Miracle Hill

REID LEHMAN

GOD WEARS HIS OWN WATCH

Published by

Miracle Hill Ministries, Inc.
2419-B Wade Hampton Blvd.
Greenville, SC 29615
www.MiracleHill.org

Designed in conjunction with

The Resource Agency
Franklin, TN

and

Susan Pottberg

Printed in the
United States of America by

Dickinson Press, Inc.
Mount Juliet, TN

Library of Congress Cataloging-in-Publication Data
Lehman, Reid
      God Wears His Own Watch/Reid Lehman
      Includes bibliographical references.
      ISBN 978-0-9770272-0-0 (pbk.: alk.paper)
      LOC # 2005932295

Dedicated to:

*My best friend and sweet wife, Barbara
My life is so rich because of
your partnership and guidance*

and

*In memory of my mother,
Mary Alice Lehman Waren
who taught me how to live in
relationship with Christ
-- entered heaven April 3, 2005*

With special thanks to
Bill Gressette and Libby Handford --
without your encouragement and support
this book would not have been published.

Preface

A dear friend, dying of cancer, told me she no longer believes God works miraculously in this age. While my heart breaks because God has not seen fit to heal her, I disagree that God is not working miraculously today. Growing up in an atmosphere focused on seeking the power of God, I saw evidence of His power as a child and have experienced it personally as an adult.

While I have seen God work, I often panic because He seems late. Sometimes when I think He must act now, I see nothing visible at all. Perhaps the "disconnect" between what I expect and what He does is normal considering He's God and I'm not. Daniel 4:35 says, "He does as He pleases with the powers of heaven and the peoples of the earth." God works and acts on behalf of His children, but we can't control how He answers our prayers, and we certainly cannot control His timing. Yes, He still works today, but God wears His own watch.

The purpose of this book is to recount and celebrate miraculous and unusual ways in which God intervened in a ministry to the homeless and has taught me to trust Him. His unexpected initiatives have often disrupted our schedules, but His answers have been amazing. May these accounts encourage you in your walk with God and embolden you to ask for more of God's presence and power.

God is still at work visibly today. *For proof, read on...*

Table of Contents

❧ ONE ❧

Where Is the Lord, the God of My Father?

The spring of 1985 brought me a dilemma greater than any I had ever experienced. I desperately needed to know that the God who had carried my father, Gerald Lehman, through his ministry would reveal the same power through me.

Elisha found himself in this position when God chose him to be successor to the prophet Elijah. In 2 Kings 2, Elisha asked his predecessor, a man of incredible spiritual power, for a double portion of His Spirit so he could do God's work. Elijah promised Elisha he would receive this double portion of His spirit if he witnessed Elijah's departure. With great emotion, Elisha watched the chariots of fire sweep Elijah up into heaven. Elisha picked up the cloak that had fallen from Elijah's shoulders. When he came to the Jordan River, he asked, "Where is the Lord, the God of Elijah?" and struck the river with the cloak. The water parted for his passage, and he crossed with the assurance that God's power, the power manifested through Elijah, was now his.

Now more than ever, I needed the power God had given my father, Gerald.

One of Dad's heroes, George Mueller, of 19th Century England, cared for orphans solely through the power of prayer. By the time of his death Mr. Mueller was supporting several thousand orphans in that manner. In chapel services at Miracle Hill Children's Home, Dad frequently told of God's provision for Mr. Mueller just as it was critically needed. He told that on one occasion — when there was nothing for breakfast, Mr. Mueller had the tables set, with children standing at them, waiting for

God to supply. Just at breakfast time, there was a knock at the door. A baker who had been unable to sleep felt led by God to get up at 2:00 a.m. to bake bread as his donation for the children. At the same meal, a milk cart broke down in front of the orphanage and the milkman donated his fresh milk so he could empty his cart and repair it.

And, just as in the Mueller stories he recounted, Dad saw that provision in his ministry. For twenty years my father had led the work of Miracle Hill Children's Home and the Greenville Rescue Mission. While finances always seemed tight, and the work operated on a shoestring, no one ever lacked the essentials. No matter how uncertain our finances during Dad's tenure; God always provided, a number of times in ways that could only be considered miraculous.

But a great testing began in 1984 when my father was diagnosed with terminal liver cancer. Over the next six months, his participation in the day-to-day leadership of Miracle Hill diminished along with his health. By February 1985, Dad was incapacitated, primarily confined to his home and unable to lead the ministry. He wondered if the ministry could continue when God took him home.

I assumed Miracle Hill's Board would appoint me Executive Director, but I shared some of Dad's misgivings about the future. Even if Dad hadn't been known and respected, he looked like a leader — his hair was now snow white. Although thirty years old, I looked five years younger and still had a problem with acne. I was thin, accentuating the prominence of my Adam's apple. I saw myself as an energy-filled decision-maker; others saw me as impatient and impetuous. I felt comfortable managing the business of the ministry, but I understood little about fundraising and knew few of the donors who had befriended my father for more than 25 years. I found myself asking, "Where is the Lord, the God of Elijah? Where is the Lord, the God of my father?"

The months of February, March, and April were somber and frightening. Spending usually outstrips income early each year, and this spring was no exception. My energy was divided between caring for my young children, helping care for my father, and trying to provide daily leadership. I should have been calling on contributors and raising needed funds, but lack of time and not knowing how to fundraise held me back.

Things seemed almost manageable until April. One weekend I realized that on Thursday, less than one week away, taxes and other obligations of approximately $8,000 were due. I did not have the relationship with contributors to ask for special gifts to cover this huge sum. Dad was praying for grace to cope with his constant pain and the weakness that now kept him bedridden. I couldn't add to his burden by sharing this need with him. If Dad had been in good health, it would have seemed simple enough. He would have called a special prayer meeting to pray the money in. But Dad could not pray with us for this. Could I expect God to answer my prayers as He had answered my father's?

I confess I was afraid. I had brashly assumed that I understood leadership. Now that it was thrust upon me, I didn't know if I could make it work. I already knew how bountifully God had provided for the ministry. So why did I lack faith to expect God to provide when He had so wonderfully provided through the years? Why could I acknowledge God's provision to others but doubt its availability to me?

Perhaps I tended to see the best side of others who had led the work. Weren't they spiritual giants who had a right to expect God to bless them? I often disappointed myself. I suppose I thought I was unworthy of that kind of provision. And it's true, I am unworthy, just as everyone trying to do God's work is unworthy. But the Christian life is not about earning God's grace. The Christian life is about living in God's wonderful grace. We aren't worthy — that's the point! God still wants to provide our needs if we'll only trust Him.

Seeking the face of God seemed to be the thing to do. And so, in spite of my fear and a sense of hopelessness, I decided to follow Dad's example. On Monday of the week the $8,000 was due, I gathered the staff to pray. A prayer meeting was held at the mission most mornings, but this session focused specifically on these taxes. Few gifts came in the mail that day. We held another special prayer meeting on Tuesday. We prayed fervently and then went to check the post office. There were few gifts. On Wednesday, we prayed once again with no visible results.

My emotions were mixed: fear, faith, and curiosity. I was afraid I wasn't spiritual enough to draw down God's supply. My faith in God had been built as He had answered prayer for Dad on other occasions. I was curious to see if this formula would work for me, or if I would somehow have to work "on my own." Please don't misunderstand. I didn't think I could do it on my own, but I honestly wondered if the power of God would help us who were trying to carry the work forward. Would God provide for Miracle Hill's needs under my leadership?

Elisha was clearly named by God as Elijah's successor. While I felt God had been preparing me for the role of Dad's successor, I really needed reassurance that He wanted me to carry the ministry forward. Although Miracle Hill's Board expressed their public support in naming me as successor, I found out much later that many of them were concerned about whether I was up to the task.

The payment was due at 2:00 p.m. on Thursday. That morning, we prayed again and checked the post office. No, there was no money to pay the bill. We had another special prayer meeting after lunch and checked the post office again. Nothing! I was crushed and disappointed. I was also embarrassed; I had told the staff the Lord would supply the need. Our confidence in

Miracle Hill's future was shaken, and I felt my leadership was in question. With frustration and some fear, we borrowed funds short-term from our bank to meet the obligation. On Friday, we again gathered and had a special time of prayer for the need. I didn't feel that borrowing the money had really been an answer to prayer. I was quite disappointed that God had let us down. We had prayed and done everything we knew to do, but God had not answered.

Until Dad became too ill to continue, either he or Morris Hallford, Director of the Children's Home, led the weekly Sunday services in the campus chapel. I had stepped into Dad's rotation and planned to preach at the Children's Home on Sunday. As I prepared, I found myself studying Psalm 34. I focused particularly on verses four and five: "I sought the LORD, and he answered me; he delivered me from all my fears. Those who look to him are radiant; their faces are never covered with shame." *Their faces are never covered with shame!*

I had been feeling ashamed because I had put my faith in God and told others to do the same, and He had not "come through." Tears came to my eyes as I studied the message, but I also felt excitement and joy. While still puzzled over the events of the previous week, I no longer felt ashamed. I had no reason to be. We had done everything before God we knew to do. On Sunday I challenged our staff to claim this promise from the Word of God, "As we look to Him we can be radiant: our faces need never be covered with shame. He can and does answer our prayers." As I chose to believe that Scripture given that weekend by God, my newfound hope was a direct gift of encouragement from the Lord.

On Monday at our prayer time, we reminded the Lord once again of the need. The discouragement was gone, but we remained puzzled. That morning a local attorney who served on our Board, called me to his office and gave me a check for more than $29,000! We do not know, even today, the source of this gift -- a donor who chose to remain anonymous. Because we did not make our need known, even to our Board, we believe the donor was unaware of the need. That gift, then the equivalent of nearly three weeks' operating expenses for the ministry, more than covered the needed payroll taxes and provided an extra cushion through the spring.

Yet even this response did not allay our concerns. Many wondered if the ministry of Miracle Hill could survive the death of my father. Deeply concerned, Dad asked God for a sign as his illness progressed. "God, send a million dollars this year to show me the ministry will continue." Dad's request seemed unreasonable and unlikely to the rest of us. Miracle Hill's annual budget then was approximately $600,000, and a million dollars had never come to the ministry in a year.

At the end of May 1985, a long-time friend and contributor, Frank Clinton, came to visit my father. Mr. Clinton, a bachelor in his 80s, was a retired school teacher from Campobello, South Carolina. He lived in a four-room house with a heater in one room. His twenty-year-old car had quit functioning recently, so he asked a nearby pastor to drive him to my parent's house. When he arrived, he shared his sympathy with my family, and then went in to visit my father. He asked Dad if Miracle Hill Children's Home had any special needs. My father said he hoped one of Miracle Hill's old concrete-block dormitories could be replaced with an attractive, individual cottage that could be used as a prototype for other cottages.

Mr. Clinton asked, "Will $100,000 be enough to help you reach this goal?"

With a weak grin, my father said, "It sure would."

The next week Mr. Clinton sent a check for $100,000, and it was sufficient to construct the 2,800 square-foot Clinton Cottage.

My father died soon after that in July 1985. Although his million-dollar request was not granted before his death, the check from Mr. Clinton assured him God was blessing and the work would continue. Dad died in peace.

I have the joy of telling you that for the 12 months ending December 1985, the ministry received more than a million dollars in income for operations and capital improvements! An unexpected and generous gift from an estate helped us reach the goal. Although it hadn't even been my prayer, I saw that answer to my father's prayer during a year when I really needed to know God's blessing would continue.

The cottage donated by Mr. Clinton was only a beginning. Two years later, we completed and dedicated Vause Cottage, a beautiful 4,000 square-foot cottage. Within five years, God had provided a way to renovate or replace each of the structures that housed the children of Miracle Hill.

I've often wondered what God would have done if I had reacted differently because I was embarrassed. What if I had quit praying? What if I had become bitter? What if I had given up? For me, many times God's greatest gifts have come only after it seemed too late. Deadlines for both the $8,000 needed for taxes and the million dollars requested by my father seemed to pass with no tangible evidence that God was going to provide. In both cases, God waited until after our human deadlines. He did His good work in our hearts, watched us trying to react with faith and dependence on Him, and then graciously provided beyond our needs.

Faith is a spiritual gift, given in greater measure to some than to others, according to 1 Corinthians 12:9. I had always seen faith as a mysterious commodity. Either you had it or you didn't. If God wanted you to exercise it, He would give it to you. If you see faith this way, you shouldn't start anything unless you know you have sufficient faith to go forward.

I now see things differently. As I've practiced faith, as I've seen God do the miraculous, I am convinced that sometimes I am to act by faith even if I don't feel any faith. If I am convinced I am following the Lord and doing, as best I know, what He has called me to do, then I need to act, even if I don't feel I have much faith. It is right to call a prayer meeting and pray as if God will meet the need even if you feel a little hopeless inside. We must keep doing what we believe God has called us to do, even if we feel horribly embarrassed and fear it's not going to work out. Courage is not a lack of fear; it's acting in spite of fear. For me faith usually does not always involve full confidence; sometimes it involves moving forward even when I'm terrified that somehow I've missed it. Perhaps it can be said, "Faith is doing what God told you to do and not having a 'plan B' to fall back on in case it doesn't work."

Psalm 91:7 says, "A thousand may fall at your side, ten thousand at your right hand, but it will not come near you." I think if a thousand people had just died on the left of me and ten thousand had just died on the right of me, I'd be very worried — even if I somehow found the courage to keep following the Lord through the middle of a battle like that. And so, many times, my actions have reflected faith in God's supply even when I knew in my heart that we were unworthy. On many of those occasions, God has seemed to be late. But based on the doubts I harbored at the time, He shouldn't have shown up at all! Then, perhaps to prove that it's all about His grace, He shows up and supplies the need generously. Whether it is for wisdom or to supply our physical needs, James 1:5 says that He never finds fault with us for asking.

TWO

My Father's Crisis of Belief

My crisis of belief was not the first one for a leader at Miracle Hill. My father moved our family onto the property that became Miracle Hill Children's Home when I was three years old. Our history there has been one of constant dependence on God's supply. One special gift from the Lord came in 1959, . . . when I was five. There was little money or credit, and the pantry had been emptied while preparing the supper meal for more than 100 children and staff. Everyone had enough to eat that evening, but Slim Kotcher, our cook, had not been able to go to the store, and there was insufficient food for breakfast.

Following supper, the staff and children gathered in the Miracle Hill campus chapel to tape the radio broadcasts they produced each week. They also took time to pray and ask God to provide breakfast the next morning. While rehearsing, they were interrupted by a knock at the door of the chapel. Members of a Pickens–area church had collected groceries for Miracle Hill Children's Home. They had planned to bring the food the following week, but the trucks they borrowed needed to be back in service by Monday morning. They apologized for interrupting the "church service," but they wanted to unload their trucks and head home. Excited, our staff stopped the rehearsal, acknowledged God's answer to prayer, and unloaded several pickup trucks full of food!

God provided on many occasions in those early years, but those early answers to prayer took place under a different leader. In 1966, Tom Kirk, "Brother Tom," leader of the ministry for ten years, left the organization and moved away. Under Tom's leadership, the ministry's annual expenses had grown from about $16,000 to more than $200,000. The number of clients in daily care grew from about 20 men and women to nearly 200 men, women, and children, and that rapid growth came with a price. When Tom left, Miracle Hill was more than $400,000 in debt, much of the money due within 90 days. (To give an idea of how huge a sum this was in those days, we'd have owed almost $2.4 million in today's dollars!) The debt was nearly two times the *annual* operating expenses of the ministry in 1966. Dad, too, asked, "Where is the Lord, the God of Elijah?"

Things seemed almost hopeless. Closing the ministry was probably the most rational approach. But there were clients in our shelters, especially children, who really needed the care they were receiving. Instead, the Board decided to try to continue. My father, who had served as an assistant director, was appointed Interim Director, while the Board continued talking to Mr. Kirk, hoping he might return.

There were dramatic contrasts between Dad and his predecessor. Exceptionally charismatic, Tom, then in his forties, was impressive in his personal presentation. About 5' 8" tall, his ruddy complexion was a startling contrast to his blond, almost–white, crew cut hair. Plump, but not offensively so, Tom dressed professionally in fashionable clothes that fit well. Tom always looked good: neat clothing, fresh haircut, manicured hands. His voice was rich and compelling.

A master salesman and showman, Tom knew how to package the ministry in a way that appealed to the hearts of others across the social spectrum. He was the only person we knew who could play the piano in a honky–tonk style and make it sound spiritual. No one was more enthusiastic. When playing for the choir, if Tom ran out of keys during a run on the keyboard, he would bang on the sides of the piano! The children in the choir would have broken their vocal cords rather than let Brother Tom down. Tom incited everyone around him to enthusiasm. He even coined a new word, "*spizerintum*," defined as unstoppable, indomitable passion for getting things done, and had a staffer draw a banner of a grasshopper on roller-skates to help charge all of our batteries. When things were tight, Tom could always find a way to get the organization by for a little longer.

Gerald Lehman made a more subdued first impression. Dad, then 35, was 5' 10" tall, with brown hair and blue eyes. His hands were rough from the necessity and relaxation afforded by physical labor. He wore business dress, but his clothes were more rumpled, less fashionable, and had often been acquired in the Miracle Hill Thrift Store. Although physically strong, Dad had a large stomach from stress, long hours, and sampling too often in the mission's kitchen before coming home for supper.

My father was a man of integrity and intelligence, but he was soft-spoken, and less assertive than Tom. Although strong in faith and personal sacrifice, he wasn't a salesman. Dad didn't know how to excite his coworkers or the ministry's supporters. Dad could not solve ministry problems through strength of personality, but he did know how to pray. When he wasn't praying, he worked long hours doing all he could.

Although Dad was respected, Board members must have wondered if he was an adequate person for the task. But when it became clear that Tom would not return, the Board appointed Gerald Lehman as Executive Director in the spring of 1967. Their concerns were justified. Gerald probably wasn't up to the task, humanly speaking, but he was a willing channel for God's power.

Gerald and other staff leaders, Mae Harlow, Tommy Shoemaker, Morris Hallford, and Ed Malloy, scrambled daily, trying to meet the most critical obligations while praying God would supply all the needs. Day-to-day survival was the operative goal for months. While the $400,000 debt was staggering, no facilities were closed, and no clients were sent away. It seems unbelievable from today's perspective, but not one meal was missed and the lights were never shut off. No one, staff or client, lacked the necessities of life — my father served a God who provided for us.

Dad went to Miracle Hill's creditors with five and ten-dollar bills saying, "This is all I can pay now. But you'll get paid back." He didn't avoid creditors when they called, and he tried to deal with them squarely, giving many of them confidence the ministry was on the right track. Most creditors proved very patient until the ministry could pay them.

There were many "just-in time" answers to prayer. Because nearly all food was donated, it was a constant struggle to ensure balanced and nutritious meals. The staff believed it was essential for good health that the children receive milk at every meal. For years Pet Dairy of Greenville supplied milk to the Children's Home. Although they contributed milk when they could, and gave us a good price on what was purchased, the milk bill for 160 children was a sizable part of the budget.

Miracle Hill, as you might expect, did not have a good credit rating at the time. The management at Pet Dairy was understandably cautious about our account. They were willing to extend credit if the ministry could be completely caught up at regular, agreed-upon dates. Pet Dairy kept their side of the bargain, but in March 1967, Miracle Hill was more than two months behind. Kindly, but firmly, the Pet Dairy representative informed us the back bill had to be satisfied before he could send any more milk. A date was set by which this bill of $750 had to be paid. Through the week before the milk bill was due, my father and the staff prayed that God would supply. On the day of the deadline, the funds were still not available.

That afternoon, a man my father did not know came to my dad's office at the mission and asked to speak with him. He was a young man, barely out of his teens, and he had evidently just completed his shift work in a nearby textile mill, for he had lint and cotton dust in his hair and on his old clothing.

Dad greeted him, and the young man sat down, initially, in silence. Dad finally asked, "How can I help you?"

The man began to cry, and he took out his billfold and removed five twenty-dollar bills and laid them on the desk. He hesitated a long minute, then dug out another five twenties, then five more, and another five. With more hesitation, the young man put another five twenties on the pile, five more, then five more. Lastly, he then took out five ten-dollar bills. Slowly and deliberately, he had counted out $750! There were no words as he counted. The only sound was that of tears dripping onto the paper bills.

Overwhelmed at God's provision, Dad asked, "What brought you here today? Why did you give this specific amount of money?"

Slowly the young man answered, "The Lord talked to me this morning and told me to take this money to the Rescue Mission. He told me they need it." Then he added, almost as an afterthought, "I was saving money to buy a car."

There was no earthly way this visitor could have known the Children's Home needed exactly $750 that day. No member of the staff knew him or had seen him before. He refused to give his name; he was just obeying God's direction to bring that money "for the care of the children." He didn't want a receipt for his gift. He walked away, and none of the staff ever saw him again.

Somehow, miraculously, through gifts like that, the ministry made it through that critical year. In August 1967, a Board member, Algie Sutton, made a challenge to the Board and the ministry. If the Board would raise at least $25,000 toward the repayment of the debt by year-end, Mr. Sutton would give a matching $25,000.

Twenty-five thousand dollars? By the end of the year? Impossible! But I remember the excitement the staff felt that someone had taken a concrete step to encourage progress. Prayers of thanksgiving mingled with prayers of petition to complete the matching amount. The total raised by the November Board meeting was only $11,130, and it now seemed very unlikely we could raise the full $25,000.

Mr. Sutton made it clear that if we did not raise $25,000 by the deadline he would feel no obligation to give his $25,000. How harmful we felt this would be to our faith to be offered hope and then have it dashed! The Board and staff kept praying.

During this period, F. A. Lawton, a long-time member of the Board, asked Mr. Sutton, "What if we raise more than $25,000?"

Mr. Sutton said, "I'll match everything you raise, up to $100,000." He and everyone else had a good laugh about that—how could we raise $100,000 when we couldn't even raise $25,000?

But the Lord, the God of Elijah, was also the God served by those who worked at Miracle Hill. And the staff, in addition to their prayers, gave as sacrificially as they could to this project. Gifts from staff, most of whom made less than $75 per month, totaled $4,000. Those who had no cash donated current or past due payroll checks. Just before Christmas, God seemed to open the floodgates of heaven. Gifts began pouring in, some from long-time friends, and many from people who had never given before. By the time the last letters postmarked December

31 arrived, more than $104,000 had been received toward the matching goal! True to his pledge, Mr. Sutton wrote a check to the ministry for $100,000.

God continued to keep the doors open and provide for the needs. A fund drive in 1969 bore fruit, and by the end of 1969, two and a half years after Brother Tom left Miracle Hill, the ministry had paid all outstanding obligations. Thereafter, the ministry ended nearly every calendar year with its debts paid. The God who enabled Elijah to do remarkable miracles was the God that Dad served, and God did keep supplying for the ministry.

THREE

Must I Choose between Ministry and My Wife?

I sat in my father's office one day in August of 1976, and I thought my heart would break because I knew what I was going to say would cause him great pain.

"Dad, I'm so sorry to have to tell you, but Barbara and I are leaving the work at Miracle Hill."

My father didn't cry easily. Only one other time in my life I had ever seen it — during an invitation in a church service when I was a teen. Now at the age of twenty-one, crying certainly wasn't in my job description, but both of us wept as I blurted out my news. Not only did I feel a personal calling to serve there, but I also knew my father needed my help and cherished our working together.

"Can you tell me why?"

"Barbara and I are in constant conflict, Dad, and it all seems to center around our work here at Miracle Hill. She doesn't think I can find a good balance between my obligations at work and my obligations to her. She feels I care too much about what others think of me."

"Can you fix that?"

"I'm not sure."

"Well son, your first obligation is to her."

Although I didn't get it at the time, as I look back, it's not surprising Barbara felt that way. We lived under a magnifying glass. Our tiny first home, just across from the campus chapel, was one of the more visible structures on campus. She was only twenty. We lived among staff who were giants in faith and self-sacrifice. We both lacked spiritual maturity, but she sensed more than I did the concern of those around us. "Was Reid wise to marry this kid from the wrong side of the tracks?"

Barbara was a committed believer. She loved serving others, but her free spirit chafed at some of the rules. Bob Jones University has always been known for strict standards, but I had enjoyed my relative freedom while a student there compared with the environment of the Children's Home. In Barbara's mind, Miracle Hill's prohibitions seemed to define spirituality as only keeping a set of rules, rather than having an intimate, joyous relationship with the Lord.

I, too, had grown up at the Children's Home, but as the son of the director. Even as a child, I always felt like part of the ministry. All of my friends growing up were children from broken homes or staff children. I completed twelve grades in the on-campus school, and often sang in one of the children's choirs, presenting the work in supporting churches.

And, it wasn't just a place to live: my work was needed. I was fired from my first job working in Miracle Hill's greenhouse when I was nine. (I couldn't be depended upon to show up for work.) But after that, I held several other student jobs and acted more responsibly. I was a dishwasher and kitchen aid, grass cutter, maintenance assistant, and caretaker for farm animals. The winter of my sixteenth year, I supervised a crew of other students clearing trees and brush so a road could be cut around the side of a hill. Not only did we cut up a lot of trees, but also the students I served with grew in emotional maturity. They developed a strong work ethic, and their behavior outside of work improved.

With that wonderful experience; I was hooked. I felt my life's calling was to serve at Miracle Hill.

Also, a fascinating girl came to live at the Children's Home the year I was in the eleventh grade. My favorite color was brown, and this attractive ninth grader had shoulder length brown hair and deep brown eyes. At 5' 7", more athletic than any girl I'd seen, she outplayed most boys in basketball, baseball, and softball. Barbara's quick wit put me in my place with ease. Well-adjusted, responsibility fit her well. And this incredible girl became interested in a skinny boy with a lot of acne and no fashion sense. We dated for five months. Then as I made plans for college, I broke up with her. (I didn't yet understand her value.) Barbara seemed to get over me quickly. She flourished at the Children's Home and rejoined her family for her senior year of high school.

From the campus in the foothills, I commuted to Greenville daily for four years, completing a business degree at Bob Jones University. Meanwhile, I supervised the maintenance program at the Children's Home. I was needed, and I enjoyed the variety and the challenge of finding ways to fix broken buildings and equipment with little or no resources.

In June 1974, just after my sophomore year, a familiar face reappeared on campus. Barbara joined the staff as a housemother for girls under the age of eleven. One of the youngest housemothers ever, she had more energy than anyone expected. She took the girls camping and killed the copperhead that came to join them. Although it wasn't her job, she would jump on the tractor to help cut grass. Our dates started early, 5:30 a.m., Saturday mornings. Since the cook, had little time off, I cooked Saturday breakfast so he could sleep in. Barbara's girls were still asleep, and with another staff member in their dorm, she could often join me. Those early dates may have preserved the health of all Miracle Hill's children. I had no business with a skillet in my hand.

And Barbara and I kept seeing each other. I think she liked being with me. I hope she didn't see me just so she could drive the front-end loader, the backhoe, and all of the tractors. I invited her to go shooting. I had borrowed a twelve-gauge, and like a little boy I wanted to see her face when she felt the heavy recoil. She made her first shot, grinned wide and kept shooting. I tried not to wince at the recoil that day as I pulled the trigger.

We both cared about people that were hurting, and we liked serving at Miracle Hill. She was a Christian, and the most exciting woman I knew! She had an uncommon resilience in surviving and overcoming adversity. I fell in love with her with all my heart, and I wanted her to be my wife—which was enough.

Barbara and I married, August 1, 1975, just before my senior year of college. I continued overseeing maintenance. Since a newlywed doesn't normally live in the dorm with the children, Barbara began working in the kitchen, helping Mrs. Wise provide three hot meals to more than 150 children and staff each day.

It was a great first year! We were busy but had fun. One of our favorite activities was to sleep in on Saturday mornings, and then lie in bed for a couple hours watching cartoons. (Don't we change, as we grow older?) My grade average went from "B" to an "A" with what seemed like less work on my part. But everything changed the month I received my degree. All newlyweds have disagreements, but ours became intense. The problem seemed structural—our presence at Miracle Hill seemed to factor into every discussion. Barbara could not bring herself to ask me to leave. She knew how important it was to me to work at Miracle Hill. But she was unhappy.

Because Barbara seemed to share my dream of serving at Miracle Hill when we married, I felt betrayed. After all, I reasoned, God had called me to serve at Miracle Hill so that was where we belonged. But the conflicts were so sharp, I feared our marriage would not survive if we stayed. I had married Barbara wholeheartedly convinced marriage was forever. Had I been tempted to leave her for the sake of the ministry, I knew I could not minister effectively after a divorce. After all, how could I ever help someone through a time of deep temptation when I couldn't even save my own home?

"God, what are You doing?" I prayed. "Why didn't you give me the wisdom to marry someone who would support Your call in my life?"

It has seemed easier through the years to trust in God's provision for the needs of His ministry than to trust His provision for my personal needs and my future. Somehow it seemed more spiritual! Of course God cares about orphans and the homeless and will do miraculous things to provide for their needs, but I thought He might not care to get involved in my personal affairs. Wouldn't it be selfish to expect God to speak to me directly?

I began to believe I had married poorly and had lost my chance to serve in ministry. I saw the problem only as between Barbara and me; and I could not see God's hand in the situation at all.

I asked God for forgiveness for leaving the ministry I felt He had called me to. Snelling and Snelling Employment Agency became my hope to find a different job. I thought I'd take any job that allowed me to move out of the state, but turned down a job with K-Mart Women's Wear! I knew I had no fashion sense. The next offer came from 84 Lumber, to serve as a manager trainee in Miami, Florida.

As I accepted the offer, I reiterated to Barbara that she came first in my life. I was willing to give up the work I loved to prove she really was my first priority. "I promise," I told her, "I won't make you feel bad about our leaving the mission." Then I warned her, "But, Barb, moving won't fix the problems between us. Your dissatisfaction will continue because it's inside of you; it's not what I do."

I was wrong, dead wrong. As soon as we moved, our marriage stabilized. We quit making life choices based on the expectations of others. We began building a healthy marriage, based on mutual respect and a deep love for God and each other. My tomboy sweetheart began learning to sell lingerie at Sears, and I applied myself to sell lumber in a city of concrete-block houses. We were careful not to let the work harm our relationship. For our three months in Miami, we attended a big church where no one knew us, so no one there had any expectations of us.

When I was transferred to Orlando, we joined Brush Arbor Baptist Church. At this church of fewer than a hundred people, we were welcomed as equals. But that time we had determined our personal standards for living, and the church's position was close to our own. Not only did Barbara feel freed from the disapproving judgment of others, she felt welcomed as a partner in ministry and a valued member of the congregation. We flourished spiritually and in our marriage.

In the fall of 1977, one year after we had left Miracle Hill, to our surprise, 84 Lumber sent me back to manage their Greenville store. We became active at Summit View Baptist Church and developed some lifetime friendships. Jim Cannon, our pastor, was a masterful expositor of Scripture. Barbara and I continued to grow in our understanding of Scripture and our relationship with Jesus Christ.

We were glad to be living again in the upstate with both sets of our parents, and we enjoyed being with them. Dad seemed over his disappointment at my leaving, and I began developing a relationship with him as his adult son, instead of his employee. Barbara and I purchased our "dream house" and were delighted when God gave us our first child, Matthew.

Through an act of will, I determined I would not get bitter about leaving the ministry, and I succeeded. In those three years, the thought of Christian service completely left my mind. I enjoyed selling lumber and managing my associates. I was earning more than I had ever imagined, and I knew I was under consideration for promotion to area manager. I was content with this new life God had given Barbara and me.

Then Barbara turned my world upside-down again. In August 1979, she asked, "Reid, have you ever thought about going back to work at Miracle Hill?"

"No, I haven't. Why do you ask?"

"Your Dad has been having health problems. He really needs some help, and with your business experience I think we could make a difference."

I hadn't thought of working at Miracle Hill for more than two years. I had truly suppressed that dream. But as soon as she suggested it, my desire to serve God at Miracle Hill awakened as strongly as ever. I wanted to serve there passionately, but what if Barbara's suggestion was just a passing fancy? Could I bear to dream the dream again, only to have it shattered when she considered realistically all the problems? "Why don't we think about it and pray about it for a month?," I suggested.

So we did. We knew we would experience a dramatic drop in income. We had been living in our "dream house" for eighteen months. It would have to go. But none of that mattered to us. By the end of September, we both felt a deep peace God wanted us at Miracle Hill. My father was thrilled. I gave my notice to 84 Lumber, and we began again at Miracle Hill on January 1,

1980. I became the Director of the Greenville Rescue Mission and Miracle Hill Industries, and Barbara worked in the office. Before long, she began ordering the groceries and supervising meal preparation for the ministry.

It took years before I understood why God had moved us away from Miracle Hill. I had thought Barbara was the cause of our leaving, but she wasn't. She was the tool God chose to use in our lives. God orchestrated that move. Yes, God wanted me to serve at Miracle Hill, but, as we now realize, we desperately needed the three years away.

It was the best education I ever received. I had never lived outside of a Christian environment. God wanted me to know how much the business world expects of its employees, for nothing more than a paycheck.

Barbara and I needed to build our marriage away from the opinions of those who had watched us grow up. My standards for the Christian life had not been my own. They had always been set by the expectations of others. Distance and time had combined to free both of us of needing the approval of other staff.

While there were godly, committed people at Miracle Hill, facilities had been built as inexpensively as possible and many were run-down from the constant shortage of funds. Business practices were inadequate, and some employees were marginal at best.

After three years away, I realized the ministry had worked so hard at being separated from the world it was out of touch with most of the world. We would have said we existed to serve people in the world and bring them to Jesus. But to most outsiders, including evangelical Christians, we were like a strange monastery. We were dedicated, but we appeared to be irrational.

Now that I could look at the ministry dispassionately, I could see some changes were vital. For instance, we had always avoided involvement with the South Carolina Department of Social Services, fearing their employees might ask us to change our Children's Home in ways that would not honor God. In turn DSS employees thought we must have something to hide since we were secretive and standoffish. It took a fresh approach and direct meetings with the state to realize we could serve God consistently and still meet state standards for the care of children.

The ministry was also segregated. My father and the Board sincerely believed that in the climate of this southern city, a homeless ministry to blacks and whites in the same facilities wouldn't work. They felt integration would be too volatile for the population we served. They feared race riots. Since there was a great need in that part of our community, Miracle Hill tried a separate shelter for African Americans. This shelter failed for lack of funding.

When I returned, some of Greenville's downtown churches wouldn't consider supporting the ministry because of its segregated stance. Our staff dreaded requests from the media for interviews. No matter how the interview began, it always ended when the reporter asked for an explanation, one more time, of Miracle Hill's racial policies.

The men and women serving in the ministry and those who governed it were deeply committed, godly individuals. None were personally prejudiced, as far as I could tell, but they were blind to the necessity of change. When I left Miracle Hill in 1976, I, too, was blind to the need for change. When I returned after living in the "real world," I was horrified that we were still segregated.

Now I could view Miracle Hill both as an insider who loved it and with an outsider's perspective that change was vital.

Had anyone who lacked a long association with the mission tried to make the changes that were needed, perhaps the leadership would not have accepted it. I was young, and perhaps I thought too highly of my own abilities, but no one could say I "didn't understand" the culture of Miracle Hill. I understood, but knew change was necessary.

I immediately began working to integrate the ministry. In May 1980, the first African American spent the night at the Rescue Mission. By 1984 we had fully integrated the staff, the Board, and all ministry facilities.

Many of the problems Barbara perceived before we left were valid concerns. I had not listened carefully to her concerns, and I often discounted them. But during my time away, I began to see how wise she had been, and I began to trust her judgment. Early in our marriage I wanted her to give me rational reasons for things she was concerned about. When she couldn't articulate clear, specific reasons for feeling as she did, I ignored her concerns as illogical—to her harm and my loss. I didn't understand God had given her womanly intuitive understanding that was beyond words or explanation. She was God's gift to give me knowledge I had no way of getting otherwise.

Just before I left the lumber company, God showed me how important it was to listen carefully, even when Barbara's reasoning seemed based on feelings, not information. Danny, a new employee working in my store, impressed me greatly. Young and energetic, I liked his "can do" attitude. Every project assigned to him was completed with dispatch. I singled him out for special attention, loaned him my truck, and wanted our families to do things socially.

However, Barbara didn't trust him and urged me not to trust him. It was the first time she had ever reacted that way to one of my business associates. She asked me not to let him borrow my truck. She didn't want to do anything with him socially. But she couldn't give me reasons. She knew nothing bad about him, only that she felt very uncomfortable about him. Manlike, I ignored her concerns and invested as much in Daniel as possible.

Quite by accident, I discovered Danny was stealing from the company by forging customer returns, and he had done so during most of his employment. He was immediately terminated and arrested. The police soon informed us that he had been released on bond and would be considered for pre-trial diversion that would allow the repayment of his debt as an alternative to going to prison.

More than a month after his arrest, as I was making a lumberyard night deposit at the bank about 9:30 p.m., a bullet struck me in the head. A 22-caliber long-rifle bullet, shot from the bushes in the back of the parking lot, came from behind my truck, striking me just below and to the left of my right ear. Flattened when it hit the truck window, the bullet fragmented when it hit my skull. Thankfully, no fragments penetrated. I initially thought a rock or a baseball bat had hit me.

Barely conscious, I hit the gas and drove to a nearby convenience store to call the police. While I waited for the police to arrive, Danny walked in, acted surprised to see me, and came over to inspect my head. Although I had no proof, I knew he was responsible for my injury. He knew my truck, our timing for night deposits, and that we normally had a substantial amount of cash. When I cried out for him to stay away, he quickly left. I had a tremendous headache, which lasted for days. As you can imagine, my deep respect for Barbara's intuition continues today!

The attempted robbery took place on October 10, just ten days after we had made the decision to go back to full-time ministry. Thankful my life was spared, I've always wondered what might have happened if I had told God "no" about returning to ministry.

I have always viewed myself as mature for my age, which may or may not be true. I defined maturity as rising above the irritations that bother others. I don't get offended easily. I prosper under adverse circumstances. Growing up in a Children's Home fostered a low tolerance for crybabies. Though being able to ignore problems that derail others can be a strength, it can also be a weakness in leadership. Many issues, which I ought to confront, I have ignored because they didn't bother me.

God gave me a wife who is far more sensitive than I am to things going on around me. She is the one who often demands a reaction when my "maturity" would do nothing at all, and I praise Him for His gift.

So I learned to trust that God knew what He was doing as He changed the course of my life through conflict with Barbara. But there were many more lessons God would have to teach me in this walk by faith. Next, I had to learn whether or not God would provide for my personal needs.

❧ FOUR ❧

My Heavenly Father Knows What I Need

When Barbara and I went back to work at the mission, we felt confident God would bless our ministry. But God wanted to teach us to trust Him for our personal needs as well.

I knew God's promises in Matthew 6:25–33 about not taking thought for tomorrow, and they were wonderful theories. But, now they are precious promises. I have joy and assurance. God says that if He clothes even the little poppies in the field and cares about the little birds, certainly He will provide for those who love Him. But it was a lesson Barbara and I had to learn through some difficult experiences.

When we felt God's leading to leave 84 Lumber Company and come back to work at Miracle Hill Ministries, my income was more than I had ever imagined it could be. I earned $32,000 in salary and bonuses in 1979. I knew the home office was pleased with my work, and I expected to be promoted with an increase in salary.

Our first son, Matt, was nine months old when we returned to Miracle Hill. I worked full time, and Barbara began working in the ministry part time. Our combined salary the next year was a little over $8,000: a huge drop for us, but at the upper end of the staff salary scale. We sold our house and began making payments on a smaller one.

Survival that first year was a real challenge. I often mowed grass for neighbors on Saturday afternoons to earn money for baby formula and diapers. Bob and Cora Rennie, former customers from my work with 84 Lumber, gave us $50 monthly for several years, which provided great encouragement as we made this transition.

Although we made it safely through that first year and never lacked for anything we really needed, day-to-day living seemed hard. Staff members could eat meals with the clients at the mission. We had lunch and supper there almost daily because we couldn't afford much in the way of groceries. The mission cooks, clients themselves, seasoned everything plentifully with pepper. Barbara and I could eat almost anything, but Matt found many dishes too strong. Fortunately, other staff lived at the same economic levels, and we were sustained as much by the fellowship there in the mission dining room as by the food.

In February 1981, our personal financial needs seemed overwhelming. Barbara was expecting our second child, due in August. We had budgeted as closely as possible. Unexpected expenses had consumed our funds, and there was no grass to mow to supplement our income. We were wondering where we'd get the money for the utility and house payment due that month. Two of our closest friends and coworkers, Wayne and Karen Scott, who had less to live on than we did, gave us a bag of groceries that included toilet paper. The toilet paper stands out in our minds because we really needed it and couldn't afford it. We felt so blessed by their largess, but it also hurt to accept it. We knew things were as tight for them as they were for us.

During the morning staff prayer meetings of this last week in February, I asked a few close friends to pray with me about our family's financial need. I emerged from prayer meeting each day refreshed and full of belief that God would supply the need. But each day God seemed to be running late. Wayne Scott and I were the only ones at prayer meeting on Friday of that week. I broke down in tears, and I expressed my hopelessness and my sense of frustration that God had not "come through." Barbara and I could see no answer for our situation. Wayne prayed with me and encouraged me. Once again I left with a sense of hope, and with that encouragement I went through the day.

Upon arriving home after work, I found a check in the mail from my former employer, 84 Lumber. Fourteen months after I left their employment, they sent a check for more than $1,000 to cover the taxes they estimated I would owe on a vacation trip I had won as a performance bonus two years earlier. The timing of the check, as best I could tell, made no rational sense. The lumber company was generous with their employees, but I could see no obligation they would have to former employees. If they really owed it, they would have undoubtedly sent it a year earlier, but God waited to deliver it until we had been driven to understand we had no recourse of any kind except simply to trust Him.

Since our income was so low in 1980, we owed little income tax. All of the check from 84 Lumber could be used on current needs, allowing us to catch up financially, and preparing us financially for Andy's birth in August.

Through this incident and many, many others, God convinced us He really did care about our personal needs.

In 1983, when Matt was four and Andy was almost two, our resources continued to be scarce. We could afford only one car, although we frequently went in different directions. Whoever was caring for the children would drive our 1978 Toyota Corolla, with car seats for the boys. The other would drive an old 175cc Honda motorcycle purchased from the Miracle Hill Thrift Store. You can imagine how difficult it was some days for both of us to meet our schedules.

That summer, Don Hummel, a former Miracle Hill Children's Home teacher, died. He had had a profound impact upon my life while I was a student in junior high, creating in me a thirst for knowledge and a life–long love of learning. I wanted very much to honor him by attending his funeral. He was to be buried in Seneca, which was about an hour away from the Children's Home.

I donned my one good dubious rose–colored suit, which I had acquired from the Miracle Hill Thrift Store. Leaving the car with Barbara, I rode the motorcycle half an hour to my parent's home and planned to ride with them to the funeral. About ten minutes from their house, a drenching cloudburst hit. I arrived at my parents' home soaking wet. We had a few extra minutes, so I took my clothes off and threw them in the dryer. The dryer had its intended effect—my suit was no longer wet—but the heat also drew out the ends of the horsehair in the fabric of my suit coat! I'll never forget my sense of helplessness and frustration as I sat in the back of my parents' car and pulled the horsehair out of my coat, trying to make it presentable! The coat was ruined, and by the time we got to the funeral, it was completely limp.

As I pulled those horsehairs, I had an animated conversation with the Lord. "Lord, it's just not fair. I'm trying to serve You. This is the only good suit I have. I wouldn't have gotten wet if we had a second car. I have to say I really don't appreciate the way you are treating me!" I didn't hear God respond.

After the funeral, I went through the receiving line to speak to Patti Hummel, Don's widow. I heard her voice change from the way she'd spoken to others. Looking me right in the eye, she said, "Reid, I don't wish to offend you, but Don asked if I would give you his clothes. Would you give me your address so I can mail his clothes to you?" I was puzzled. It seemed an odd way for God to answer the accusations I'd made against Him. How did I know if Don's clothes would even fit me?

Sure," I answered. I gave her my address, but I went home still thinking God didn't care, as much about my needs as I thought He should.

Two weeks later two boxes arrived with a variety of clothing, all in excellent condition. Two beautiful suits fit me perfectly. There were also dress shirts, dress pants, and other items of clothing I could use. It was then that I heard God's answer to my diatribe. He said, so kindly, "I really do care. I will provide for your needs. You just need to wait on Me."

And God did continue providing. We never lacked anything we really needed, but there were some hiccups along the way. Hiccups? There were unexpected interruptions. As our boys grew, the small home we had purchased when I began working again with Miracle Hill seemed to get smaller. After much prayer and struggle, we put our home on the market hoping to move closer to our church, which also housed the school our sons attended and where Barbara now worked.

Our home remained on the market for seven months with few inquiries. Then, in August 1986, we discovered that a land auction would take place on the site of a former peach orchard in an ideal spot for us to build. As we returned home after that discovery, we found a note from our realtor on our kitchen table with a generous offer for our house. With the proceeds from the sale of the house, we purchased a lot and prepared to build.

God kept opening doors. With my background selling building materials, I hoped to do as much as possible of the work on our house myself. A friend who owned a heating and air conditioning company agreed to serve as the contractor-of-record for construction. Friends of Miracle Hill who owned a lumberyard agreed to provide credit for building materials. With the Board's permission, I hired Miracle Hill's construction staff to help frame the house. I took two weeks off for framing in July 1988, and then worked every possible moment of spare time that summer and fall to construct our new home.

On November 23, the Wednesday before Thanksgiving, Barbara and I were both near the end of our respective ropes. We were weary to our bones from working every spare moment on the house. The home was ready for sheetrock, so completion wasn't too far away. Yet, it still seemed we would never finish.

That morning Barbara and I had a strong disagreement, unresolved as we went separately to work. Why we fought, we can't remember — but we were worn out and irritated. Soon after I arrived at work, I received a call from Barbara telling me she was "all right" — scary words. She had wrecked a school van while taking a sixth-grade girls physical education class to McDonalds. In rain and heavy fog, she had missed seeing a large metal pole in the center of the school's driveway. The van had not missed however, and had parked itself on the pole on about a 30-degree angle. Fortunately, there were only scrapes and bruises. The fight quickly forgotten, the accident reminded both of us of our priorities.

Thanksgiving at our ministry facilities is celebrated on the Wednesday evening before Thanksgiving. That night I preached at the Greenville Rescue Mission using Romans 8:28 as my text: "And we know that in all things God works for the good of those who love him, who have been called according to his purpose." The theme of my message that night was that because of our circumstances, thanksgiving need not always be a spontaneous act of gratitude.

"When we live in hardship or suffering, thanksgiving may instead be an act of will," I said. "We determine to be thankful because God desires it and because even in unpleasant circumstances, he is working toward our good in every circumstance of life."

Seven hours later, we received a call from one of our soon-to-be new neighbors. "Is this Reid Lehman? This is Betty, over across the road from your new house. I thought you'd want to know your house is on fire."

Barbara wouldn't let me go alone. The boys were too small to leave by themselves. So the four of us arrived about 2:20 a.m. Thanksgiving Day, in time to see the roof collapse. The house was totally destroyed. As we stood there shivering from shock and the cool night air, I seemed to hear the Lord saying, "Did you mean that last night, Reid? Do you really believe that in all things I am working for your good?"

As I stood there in the darkness and thought about it, I realized I did believe that passage, and with joy I realized Barbara was as committed to it as I was. Because we had worked so hard, there were a few tears. But we could even laugh a little when Matt, then about nine, said, "Dad, didn't you want to change a few things about this house?"

Although finances were tight, we returned to our rented home, cleaned ourselves up, packed suitcases and left for the beach. We could think of no better way to celebrate Thanksgiving as a family, that day, than to go off and enjoy one another. We had a great weekend!

December brought negotiations with the insurance company, cleaning up debris and planning for reconstruction. The fire appeared to have been set, a source of concern, because I have worked with hundreds of troubled people over the years. I couldn't help but wonder if a disturbed former client had set the fire. Several years later a local pastor called to say that some young men, teens at the time of the fire, had just confessed their role in burning our house as an act of random vandalism. He didn't volunteer their names: we didn't need them. It was a relief to know it wasn't personal.

In January I contracted mononucleosis, putting me flat on my back for weeks. Although I could do little but lie in bed, it was one of the sweetest times I've ever had with the Lord. I couldn't read. I couldn't even think, but I could pray and rest in Him.

More than a month later, I returned to work at Miracle Hill for two-to-three hours daily: it was several months before I could be fully back in the office again. It took six months before I could begin manual labor. We began rebuilding that summer and celebrated our first meal living in our new home on Thanksgiving Day, 1989. And, because the insurance company had made allowance for the value of my labor, we now had a garage and some extras we couldn't have afforded before.

I can honestly say our hearts were filled with gratitude and awareness of the richness of God's grace almost equally on the day our house burned as on the day we celebrated our new home.

The following spring our pastor was leading the church through "Fifty Days of Purpose." There was a focused Bible study each week on a different area of surrender to God. One week, there was a challenge to give God a real sacrifice — something each of us personally valued. In our family devotions, I challenged my sons to give God, that week, something each really valued. I suggested that Andy give one of his favorite toys to a young family who came to our home that week for Sunday dinner. Randy, the husband, was working for Miracle Hill while training for missionary service overseas. Andy had an abundance of toys, but seemed willing to give their young children only a few of his broken ones. I was frustrated at his selfishness, when I realized that outside of our tithe, I had not given God anything of value lately.

As I thought of what I valued, God brought my prized worm gear-driven circular saw to mind. This tool, purchased at a pawnshop before starting the house, had served well during construction. I no longer needed it, although I still treasured it. After a couple-days' struggle, I called Randy and asked if he could use it. Randy's unsaved father would arrive in Greenville the next week and was planning to remodel some of Randy's home. Randy needed a saw, and this gift would help his father see God provide for their needs. As I told my sons I was going to give my saw to Randy, Andy said, "Dad I want to come along, I'll give them some of my toys." When Andy saw me give away my precious saw, he gave Randy's children several toys he valued most.

My new spiritual high lasted for about two days. I had completed the house and was transferring the construction loan to a permanent mortgage. As I totaled outstanding obligations, I realized the new home mortgage would cover all but about $3,300 of my outstanding bill with the lumberyard.

First, I complained, "Lord, I've been trying to do things right. You know I just gave you the saw I loved. Now, look at my bills. I'm pretty discouraged with this one I can't pay. It just doesn't seem fair." I didn't hear God say anything.

With a heavy heart, I called the lumberyard, told of my dilemma, and asked if I could begin paying the balance of the debt off over a period of time—hoping for at least two years to pay for it. The answer came quickly. "We want to invest in your new home. We're planning to write off the balance. You don't owe us a thing."

Immediately I was ashamed. I had just given God a saw worth about a hundred dollars—one I no longer needed. He had already led someone else to forgive me of a debt that would have taken me years to pay. And, just a few minutes earlier, I was complaining. He has been and continues to be so good to me.

FIVE

We Set Ourselves Adrift

When I was growing up I saw over and over again God's provision for the needs of our family and for Miracle Hill Ministries. While my father lived, he constantly reminded everyone under the sound of his voice of the things God had done. Frankly, I sometimes felt bored by Dad's stories and thought there was a bit of overkill in his telling them over and over!

But I was wrong.

Psalm 78 tells us that we must pass on to our children what we have learned about God's faithfulness and holiness, "what we have heard and known, what our fathers have told us. We will not hide them from their children; we will tell the next generation the praiseworthy deeds of the LORD, his power, and the wonders he has done." If we are going to pass on to the next generation anything we know about a relationship with God, we must first **tell** them about the "praiseworthy deeds," the wonderful things He has done. Secondly, they must **experience** God at work for themselves. The Hebrew word translated "to know" refers to a vital, personal experience. Thirdly, this Psalm shares the concept "our fathers have told us." We fathers must be faithful to remind our children not only that God works, but we need to interpret the experiences we have gone through together as God at work, not just happenstance. My father did it over and over again. It used to irritate me. Now that I'm older, I'm glad he did.

There came a day when I realized I had confidence in the provision and watch care of God. I knew He would take care of my needs in the future. I longed for my two sons to experience this as well. Our family prayed together for Miracle Hill's needs. My sons prayed with me for dollars for the ministry, but I saw no evidence that praying for or even hearing of God's supply had any real meaning to the two of them in their own lives. Because we did not live on campus, they would hear of God's supply but not often see it for themselves. For several years, I searched for a way to give them the experience of seeing God provide for them directly.

I finally realized that the only way I could do so was to take them into a situation where we had no resources of our own, and where we had to depend upon God to supply. I visualized it like climbing into a boat without oars and pushing out into the stream to see where God would take us. Because of my work with the homeless, I decided to take my oldest son Matt, as he turned 13, to a city unknown to us. I planned to go to a city several hours from Greenville where the street people would not know me, to live on the streets of that city for five days with no preplanned resources, to look for God to supply.

Pursuing that goal, Barbara dropped Matt and me off in the heart of Wilmington, North Carolina, on Palm Sunday, 1992. I knew nothing about Wilmington. We left the car with only the clothes we were wearing and a driver's license in my pocket to prove my identification, if I needed to. I had not shaved in almost two weeks. Matt had not cut his hair for several weeks. Both of us wore our oldest clothes. We had no money, no credit cards, no toiletries, and no food except a pack of crackers that Matt saved from lunch.

Barbara decided she and Andy would spend the time we were gone with her grandmother, who lived an hour away. Not surprisingly, she was distraught at leaving her young son exposed to the unknown for a week. She dropped us off, but she wept so hard she found it difficult to drive. She stopped on the outskirts of Wilmington and called a godly friend. Gloria prayed with her, and Barbara found the strength to leave us behind. I had assured her Matt and I would be completely safe. But, to be honest, I had hidden an envelope in my sock drawer at home with the ominous words inside, "If you find this letter . . .." While I felt confident interacting with the homeless, I knew we weren't completely safe. I wasn't sure I could stay awake to keep an eye out for danger if we had to sleep outside. Those who prey on the homeless while they sleep generally don't wake them up to ask for money. They may just hit them in the head with a brick to keep them unconscious while they search. As the car disappeared, Matt and I prayed for God's supply.

Walking down the street, we came to a maritime museum on Market Street. With empty pockets, I asked if we could do any work there to gain admittance. Admitted at no charge, we explored the museum until its closing. We asked the proprietor if there was a local Rescue Mission, and he gave us directions. We walked several blocks and found the place. It was a converted two-story house. They offered me a place to stay, but said they couldn't accept or allow children. They told us about a Salvation Army shelter nearby. We walked there and learned they had room for us.

I told the desk clerk that Matt and I were temporarily separated from our family and thought we would be able to rejoin them on the following Thursday. We ate supper, received clean linens, towels and soap, and were assigned a bunk in the men's quarters. Although Matt's bunk was above mine, he was frightened in that strange place and slept very little that first night.

On Monday we began looking for work. Most of the morning we experienced rejections, and no wonder. Why would a prospective employer want to hire a scruffy-looking man with a boy attached? However, just before noon, a contractor offered me a job pouring concrete if I would return the next morning.

We walked on to a church–sponsored soup kitchen and sat down for lunch. Matt was pretty discouraged, and I shouldn't have been surprised. As I ate my soup, I noticed he was not eating. Looking more closely, I saw he was crying.

"Dad, they put mayonnaise on my bologna sandwich! And I don't want to be here anyway!" I sensed it wasn't just the bologna sandwich; and I concluded Matt was tired and scared.

My eyes filled with tears, but I didn't know anything I could do to help him. Matt excused himself and walked, sniffling, outside the building to wait while I finished eating. After he left, one of the soup kitchen volunteers came over. "I notice your son seems to be having a hard time. Can I help?"

"I'm sorry to inconvenience you, but do you suppose you could make him a bologna sandwich without mayonnaise?"

"Sure can!" she said cheerfully. Back in the kitchen, she created a deluxe ham sandwich with lettuce, tomato, no mayonnaise, and fresh bread! She added treats and snacks and brought it all out in a brown paper bag. When Matt saw that "goodie bag," he began to brighten up—that moment became the turning point of our trip.

When I asked Matt, now serving in the Peace Corps, for permission to share the story of our trip to Wilmington, he shared new information on the emotions he had that day.

> "It wasn't necessarily the mayonnaise on the
> sandwich that put me over the edge, it was a guy
> sitting next to me who was very overweight and
> severely mentally challenged. While we were eating

I didn't take my eyes off him. Everyone that walked by him made a joke about him, and they would also pile their leftover food on his plate to make fun of his weight. He didn't say a word the whole time I watched, he just ate. When you add the mayonnaise from his sandwich running down his chin to everything that was going on around him it was just too much for me to handle. There was too much emotion. My heart was broken for this man: for these people. I grew up around people like this, but there was always a sort of protective barrier. The barrier was no longer there in Wilmington. I think for the first time that I saw the homeless as real people. That is why I started crying about the mayonnaise. It was years before I could eat mayonnaise again. Even now, when I put a little on a sandwich, I see his face."

We settled in that afternoon to relax and enjoy the rest of the week. Since we had work lined up the next day, we began to explore the waterfront. After supper, confined to the shelter's fenced walls, we talked, used a small rock as a soccer ball, talked, listened to other people talk, and talked some more. What a wonderful time of uninterrupted, unpressured time together.

On Tuesday the promised concrete work did not materialize, but we soon found work with a contractor tearing out plaster walls in an old house. We had lunch again at the soup kitchen. The contractor assured me he had work for me for the duration of our stay.

By Thursday morning I had $60 in my pocket, fresh clothing and personal toiletries. Matt and I had turned down housing and a permanent job. In fact, God answered every prayer exactly as we had prayed it during the five days. By the last day, we needed nothing for ourselves, so we prayed for a fellow shelter guest at the Salvation Army who was in danger of losing his job because he was running late. We saw God answer prayer that morning when his ride came on time for the first time.

You can imagine Barbara's relief when I phoned. We called to let her know we were all right and where to pick us up. My primary goal of the venture was to help Matt see God act in his own life in a real and personal way, but it had a secondary benefit I had not expected. Matt's twelfth year had been frustrating for him, his mother, and me. When we left on this trip, I didn't really like him very much. Of course I loved him — fathers are supposed to love their children! But I didn't really care very much for Matt. I thought he was selfish and self-centered, and I hoped he couldn't tell how I felt. I sensed he didn't care for me at all, either. He saw me as autocratic and out of touch with the real world. But by the time Barbara picked us up at the end of that week, we were deeply committed to each other. We had forged a closeness that helped us all to survive his turbulent teens. Of course we had later conflicts, but always both of us were sure of the love of the other.

Two years later, in August, just before Andy turned 13, I planned a similar experience for him in Savannah. While Barbara had allowed my excursion with Matt without strenuous objection, this time she wanted to be sure she was getting through to me. She said without a smile, "You do understand, don't you, Reid, that if you come home without our son, we are going to have a real problem in our marriage."

I answered, "I'm listening very carefully. I promise I'll bring Andy back in good shape."

"Then don't you leave a letter for me in the sock drawer that says, 'If you find this letter'"! she responded.

On a Saturday afternoon, Andy and I drove to Savannah

and left the car in long-term airport parking. I left a credit card in the car so we could pay for the long-term parking later, but I took only car keys and a driver's license with me. We hitchhiked several miles into Savannah. As we walked, I discovered some change in my pocket and left it on a manhole cover so we could arrive truly broke. A light rain turned heavy quickly, and by the time someone stopped to offer us a ride, we were soaked. The driver knew of the local Rescue Mission and took us there. They fed us supper, but the mission had a policy, just as in Wilmington, that no children could stay.

After supper, we walked about 40 minutes to find the Salvation Army. I told the intake counselor we were temporarily separated from our family and hoped to rejoin them again before the end of the week. Once again, I had a two-weeks' start on a patchy beard, a safety pin held my glasses together, and my clothes were speckled with paint. Andy's hair was shaggy, but he had been looking forward to the trip and found it hard to hide his grin of excitement.

On Sunday morning we attended a service at the Salvation Army church. The gospel was presented clearly, and the speaker was compassionate and respectful of his audience.

Since I am a director of a rescue mission myself, I took special note of this. In my stays in Wilmington and in Savannah, this was the only time we heard a presentation of the gospel. On both trips we stayed in a Christian shelter. On the first trip we ate in a soup kitchen operated by Christians, but outside of the Sunday service in Savannah, neither in the shelters nor in the soup kitchen, did anyone ever tell us of the love of Christ. People were generous with physical assistance, but no one ever met with us to ask what was broken, how we became homeless, and if we needed spiritual or emotional help. I want to be sure that never happens in the ministry I direct. What use is it to serve a man's body, which is, after all, one day going to turn to dust, and not give him the words of eternal life which will determine his eternal destiny?

After a Sunday lunch, as good as we could have received at home, we set out to explore the neighborhood. The Savannah Science Museum looked interesting. Having no funds, I offered to work around the place to gain admittance for Andy. Five minutes sweeping, a job given more to protect our dignity than to meet the needs of the museum, gained us admittance. We spent a pleasant afternoon together and returned to the shelter for supper. On Sunday evening one of the cooks invited us both back into the kitchen and gave Andy sweets and some snacks for later.

Monday, after breakfast, Andy and I began looking for work. Remembering Matt's discouragement while in Wilmington, I made a solemn prediction to Andy. We would ask for work at ten different locations, and the first nine would turn us down. But the tenth request would be granted. We began walking southwest of the shelter on Montgomery Street. At every business I asked, "Is there any work I can do for you? I'm willing to do the dirtiest job you have. You can pay me whatever you think I am worth, and if you don't like my work, you don't have to pay me at all."

As expected at the first three places we stopped, our offer was declined.

"Isn't this great, Andy?"

"What's that, Dad?"

"Only seven more requests like this and we'll have work."

"Aw, Dad."

We walked for a while in a poorer residential neighborhood, seeing no opportunity for work. When we came upon a contractor conducting a morning work meeting with his crew on the front porch of a house undergoing renovation, I made my fourth request, "Sir, do you have work for me?"

The carpenter knew that many ask for work when all they really want is money. To my surprise, he called my bluff and sent me back to the kitchen with a sledgehammer, shovel, and a wheelbarrow. My assignment was to knock down a chimney and empty the debris into a metal container in the back yard. Andy helped for a while and then explored the neighborhood while I worked.

God had provided work that morning, but we did not have any resources for lunch. We couldn't go back to the Salvation Army until supper. A shelter client had told us of a soup kitchen downtown. Shortly before noon, I finished the chimney. The contractor and his crew were working elsewhere, so Andy and I left the house and walked more than half an hour to the area where we had heard there was a soup kitchen. We finally found the address only to find a sign on the gate that said, "Closed two weeks for repairs."

Andy sat down on a park bench and wept, and so did I, sitting beside him. My tears were not from hunger but from helplessness. "Lord," I prayed silently, "it doesn't matter to me whether I have lunch or not, but I've told Andy that You will supply our needs. I would like You to give him a hamburger, fries, and a Pepsi." (Andy wouldn't touch a Coke back then!) A little roughly, I got Andy up and marched him back to the job site. In our absence, the contractor had returned bringing us each a hamburger, fries, and a Pepsi. Since we were gone, he'd eaten the hamburgers. Our lunch consisted of fries, Pepsi, and snacks Andy had brought from the Salvation Army shelter. We could have had hamburgers, too, except we went looking for lunch instead of waiting on God to deliver it!

That afternoon I used the contractor's tools to frame windows and doors—I enjoy working with my hands. Before the end of the day, my employer offered me regular work and a place to live. I promised him an answer by Tuesday afternoon, which is when I told him I had a job back in Greenville and I appreciated his offer.

By the time we left Wednesday morning, we had cash in our pockets, extra clothing, toiletries, and we had not missed a single meal. Once again, God had answered every prayer as we had prayed it. On Wednesday, with more than $50 in cash in our pockets, we took a taxi back to our car at the airport, paid the cost of the parking, and drove home again.

My Savannah experience was everything I hoped for and more. Andy saw God answer prayer every day. Both of us gained insight into the lives of other shelter guests as we heard what they say in the bunkroom when the staff aren't around. One man bragged about trading his only pair of pants for a six-pack of beer before coming to the shelter. Although my relationship with Andy had been good, the experience drew us closer together. We had come to no harm, except that we caught body lice from the bedding in the shelter. A good dose of Quell shampoo got rid of the lice when we got home.

Through these excursions, my sons and I saw God clearly answer specific prayers. There was never a time when I felt unsafe, we never missed a meal, we never slept outdoors, and my terrific wife stayed married to me even though I had put her children at risk.

Before going to Wilmington, Matt and I lived in a state of armed truce. He thought I was out of touch and unreasonable. I thought he was rebellious and spoiled. He didn't want to go to Wilmington or anywhere else with me for that matter. By the time Barbara picked us up, we were good friends. We enjoyed one another's company and gained a profound respect for each other, which we still both treasure.

Though Andy and I had a good relationship when we went to Savannah, what we experienced there drew us much closer. It built a deep reservoir of trust and mutual respect that brought us through some scary teenage years.

But best of all, my sons had not just heard *about* a God who answers prayer. They had come to know the God who answered their prayers and who delights to do so.

SIX

A Miracle Hill!

"If something's worth doing, it's worth doing right." It's a truism we often heard our mothers quote, thinking to motivate us to do our tasks better.

But if the dear people who have worked with the Greenville Rescue Mission and the Children's Home had operated on that principle, how many, many lives would have been untouched! How many children would have suffered mistreatment and hunger! Those sturdy pioneers in this ministry seemed to operate on the principle, "If something is worth doing, it's worth doing poorly until you get a chance to do it better."

They would have said, "If there is a need out there that you know is dear to God's heart, if you've prayed about it and believe He wants you to get involved, why not get started?" They asked, "What are the needs that God weeps about? How can I be used by Him to meet those needs?" Of course, we should minister in the best way possible, but sometimes we must start with whatever resources we have to meet the need God has laid on our hearts.

Today, at Miracle Hill, we consider starting a new ministry by taking extensive surveys about the need, gathering a great group of others passionate about the cause, and by waiting until the completion of a capital campaign before we actually initiate new ministry. And that is a valid approach.

However, we didn't begin that way. If our people had waited until all of the pieces were in place, the ministry might never have been started. Across the country, many of those who reach out to addicts and the homeless were destitute themselves not very long before. They know how it feels to be in need, and they know the deliverance of the Lord.

Those who began Miracle Hill were eager to help others experience His help, but they knew little about running a ministry. In fact, those who came to us, not because they themselves had needed help, but because they had a passion for those in need, often had been training for a different ministry, and God Himself interrupted their plans. My father trained in Bible college to go to New Guinea as a missionary. Instead, in the very town where he had trained, God placed him among the dregs of the city. You must understand ministry to the poor and the weak is not a prestigious calling.

In the same way, the beginning of Miracle Hill Children's Home was neither planned, nor well organized. In the 1950s, most of those who understood fundraising and how to run nonprofit organizations were running museums and fundraising for universities. Few who knew how to raise funds seemed to care about homeless children running the streets of Greenville, South Carolina. Though the Greenville Rescue Mission operated a shelter for men and women, there was no ministry or plan in place to care for children. One Sunday afternoon, in the fall of 1956, the police arrived at the Mission with a family of three children. They'd been found in a house alone, and the neighbors reported they had been left alone for several days. The police wondered if the Rescue Mission could care for these children until something else could be arranged.

Mae Harlow and Millie Carper, Bob Jones University staffers who were volunteering at the Mission that evening, accepted the children immediately and compassionately. They took them to the second floor, bathed them, fed them, and got them ready for bed. They had no formal acceptance plan to follow. There was no Board action taken to expand the ministry to care for children. Here were three woeful, neglected, and frightened children. They needed food, a safe place to sleep, a kind and gentle touch. How could Mae and Millie refuse to help them? They felt like Jesus feels toward children. They knew it would be un–Christ-like to turn them away. So staffers and volunteers cared for those three little ones. In a few months, other children, some brought by law enforcement, others from pastors or relatives, joined the first three.

Mae paid a price for her boldness in determining to meet the needs of the children. She was a professional secretary. She had never envisioned being a housemother, but she saw the need and quit her job at the university to work full time with no salary, taking care of the children. She had food and a place to stay, and she was content with that. Mae had the great joy of seeing God use her to meet the vital needs of these motherless, needy children.

But living quarters at the mission were very crowded with the children, homeless women, and some staff all living on the second floor. Mae and other members of the staff began to pray that God would provide a separate house for the children, and He did provide. The Mission purchased a house with seven bedrooms and two bathrooms, at 813 West Washington Street. Renovation of the basement provided two more bedrooms. On move–in day, a parade of 34 children and two staff walked from the Mission to their new home!

Eloise Drummond and Vivian Blough joined the staff to mother the children in these new quarters. Before long there were 58 children, and the walls were bulging again. How did they manage all those children with only two bathrooms in the place?

Miss Emmie Hicks willed her family home on Pendleton Street to the mission. This wonderful gift gave us eight more bedrooms and, glory be, five bathrooms! Girls ages six and older were moved to Pendleton Street along with Miss Eloise and Miss Vivian. Mae supervised the house at 813 W. Washington Street caring for babies, toddlers, and boys up through age 12. Vera, her office assistant, moved there with them. When she was not in the office, she assisted in the care of the children.

In 1955, even before Mae came, the mission had purchased an old farm, the boyhood home of Board member Clyde Jones, twenty miles north in the Oolenoy Community of Pickens County. The mission hoped to use it to rehabilitate men from the mission. My father, Gerald Lehman, began living on the property in 1957 with my mother, my sister, and me.

Dad had a farming background, and he was studying for the ministry. He was asked to take in alcoholics and disciple them while teaching them to farm. The ramshackle, four-room house was drafty and cramped. I think those days were hardest on Mom as she tried to find resources for her five children. A dustpan wasn't needed in the old farmhouse. When Mom swept the floor, the dirt and crumbs fell through the cracks under the house where the chickens scrambled to find anything edible. Money was always scarce, even for basic needs. One of the toughest times came when the pig fell into the well and died, diminishing both the drinking water and the food supply! A few years later, I recall asking for a snack after school. I found mustard to put on bread: there was nothing else to put into a sandwich.

Perhaps because the mission had so quickly responded to the need of abandoned children, teenage boys who had never completed school were now coming to seek care from the mission. The police brought many that they had arrested for petty (and not so petty) crimes; other boys were abandoned by their families. Since the Children's Home in town was limited to boys younger than 13, teenage boys came to the farm along with the men. The staff soon realized that these boys, grown or almost grown, had little schooling and they had a burden to help them get a good education. When the boys would get frustrated with school — and they were a long way behind, they would smart off. Sometimes they'd want to fight. When the staff won, and they always did, schooling would resume.

My father began the process of planning a curriculum and rebuilding the corncrib to make a classroom. John Macon and Morris Hallford joined the staff in 1959 to become the first teachers. In 1960, both of them married — each to a trained teacher! John's wife, Fay, was an elementary teacher. Morris' wife, Doreen, a high school English teacher, found teaching English challenging to boys with their troubled backgrounds. Thus, the ministry's Continuation School was established.

The physical climate was primitive but there was a passion on the part of everyone to share the gospel. Michael, one of those boys, wrote the following more than 40 years later:

> When I was 11 years old, my family was having a real rough time! My mother was sick and dying... when all at once, our heavenly Father stepped in and made a way for my eldest brother and me to come to Miracle Hill School! That was in 1959, and everything was just getting started! I had always heard of the love of Christ but never understood its true meaning, until early one morning I woke up and had to go to the bathroom, which at that time was in the woods behind the barn. The sun was just coming up, and I was able to see more as I walked back into the house. Everyone was still asleep except Mr. Hallford . . . my teacher and my guide . . . . He was on his knees praying . . . for God to help him be the person to us boys that he needed to be! He was calling out all our names, talking to God about each one of us! That's when I realized what real love was! . . . I later gave my heart to Christ . . . in one of the daily meetings that started our day!

With staff living in the farmhouse, only about ten boys could be housed there. As the numbers grew, some boys slept in the back of a truck body, while the staff planned for expansion. During one summer, with the aid of some Bob Jones University students, the Mission had conducted a summer camp at the farm for the children from the Children's Home. It seemed such an ideal place to rear children. Brother Tom and the Board decided that this land, twenty miles north of Greenville, would be the place to build a new building there to care for all of the children. There were only enough funds for preparing the land. The new building was started on faith.

Workmen graded the top of the hill for the new building they expected to be 20 feet x 40 feet (800 square feet). Ballard Concrete of Greenville manufactured and sold pre-stressed concrete roof trusses. Friendly to the ministry, they agreed to give extra trusses from their inventory to help build the children's building. The building was designed to make the best use of some 24 foot trusses they had offered. There was no architect, Oregon Lawton, a partner in Lawton Lumber Company, drew up tentative plans and supervised the work.

The shape and size of the building changed after an interesting philosophical discussion. Today, no one is sure where the thought originated although it was thought that the teenage boys first said it.

"We're starting by faith a building we can't pay for," the reasoning went. *"If we can trust God to give us a small building on faith, why can't we trust Him to build us a larger building on faith?"*

The enthusiastic planners contacted Ballard concrete again. They agreed to donate additional trusses. The building would now have two wings, each wing 24 feet wide and a 40 foot center section with a higher roof to be used as a multipurpose room. The total dimensions would now be 89'x 80'. At 7,120 square feet, this design would be almost 9 times larger than the original building planned!

We had the trusses, but trusses need concrete block walls. To meet that need, God stepped in and sent a remarkable woman to our aid. Mrs. Louise Smith was a pioneer in stock-car racing, a sport traditionally dominated by men! But Mrs. Smith had another passion besides stock-car racing. She had a passion to see a work established for the children. She took it upon herself to provide concrete block for the walls of the new building. Mrs. Smith was encouraged in this partly because some of the teenage boys, who used to pilfer from her husband's auto salvage yard, were now being cared for in the home, and they were clearly learning and growing. As one of the few women professional drivers ever, Louise was used to pursuing causes that seemed unlikely. (Later, she became the first woman inducted into the International Motorsports Hall of Fame!) In 1958, Louise engineered an invitation to appear on the game show, "Queen for a Day," in New York.

"What do you want to win?" the emcee asked.

"Concrete block to build a Children's Home back in South Carolina."

She returned to Greenville with funds to buy all the block needed for the building!

Groups of church volunteers came from as far away as Indiana and Virginia to help build the new facility. As they were pouring the concrete floor, storm clouds threatened a heavy rain. Not only did the concrete already poured need to be worked properly, but also more concrete needed to be poured that day, since the volunteers were going to have to return home. The workers stopped long enough to pray that God would not allow the rain to hinder pouring of the concrete. Soon after that prayer, the workers could see a solid sheet of heavy rain moving toward them, but they watched in astonishment as the thunderclouds parted right at the construction site at the top of the hill. The rain fell all around them, on both sides of the hill, then joined again at the base in force. The bottom of the hill was soaked, but there was only a light sprinkle at the top! The volunteers continued pouring and working the new concrete floor without interruption.

When Vera Wright, a secretary on staff, heard of this prayer and God's miraculous answer, she said, "This is just like a miracle hill, isn't it?" Everyone agreed, so the Children's Home and later the entire ministry became known as Miracle Hill.

Mr. Buckwalter, a blockmason from Virginia, was vacationing in Greenville with his family. He let the family vacation without him; he was heartily laying the block for the new building. Omer Samples, a mason and active volunteer with the Evansville Indiana Rescue Mission, drove hundreds of miles to give of his time. The Singer Company of Pickens mobilized dozens of employees to paint the building, inside and out, in a day. Gage and Nancy Kent, from Iowa, donated a campus sewer system. From many unexpected sources, God brought people and materials together to provide this comfortable, sheltering, safe home in the rolling hills of Pickens County. In the fall of 1959, Miracle Hall, the new children's building, was dedicated.

Those wonderful pioneers in this ministry knew it was a work worth doing. It was imperfect patchwork, without a coherent plan and plenty of flaws, but the little children who desperately needed care were nurtured, fed, clothed, and taught. They knew they were loved, and many came to know the one who said in Luke 18, "Let the little children come to me, and do not hinder them, for the kingdom of God belongs to such as these."

SEVEN

Sacrificial Pioneers

At the beginning of this book, I mentioned a difficult transition in 1966 when my father was first appointed interim director. The ministry was heavily in debt. Many of Miracle Hill's vendors refused to sell the ministry anything more on credit. Groceries had to be paid for when delivered.

Although most of the staff lived in ministry facilities and ate along with the clients in our dining facilities, all worked at personal sacrifice. There was no health insurance. The target salary was $15 per week for single staff, $25 per week for couples, with or without children. I said, "target salary" because everyone knew that utilities and food came first: paychecks were issued when and if God provided funds for them.

Twelve weeks of payroll were missed during that critical transition year. When finances began easing, Dad wrote the staff and told of his desire to somehow find money to catch up payroll. In that letter he talked of the continuing need and asked for volunteers from among the staff to forgo paychecks for some of the weeks for which they had not been paid.

Twenty years later, perusing old files, I came across a folder containing written replies from our staff during that time. I was awe–struck by the sweet, sacrificial responses. All gave one or more weeks' salary; many gave half of their twelve outstanding checks; others forgave almost the entire amount owed.

"I need three paychecks to catch up my car payments. Keep all the rest."

"We have some medical bills that are unpaid, but if you can pay me for four weeks, we can make it just fine."

"I've gotten behind on my school bill this year. If you can give me a third of what you owe me, I'll be so grateful."

Those staff were fervent about serving God at any cost. They loved the children at the Children's Home and the men and women at the Rescue Mission, but their greatest passion was to serve God.

Although we know few stories from the ministry's first twenty years, there are clear memories of God at work for the last half-century. Two staff, Mae Harlow and Vera Wright have been employed continuously by the ministry since 1957–58. My mother, Mary Alice Lehman Waren went to be with the Lord April 3, 2005. It seemed wise to capture some of their memories and our Miracle Hill story before memories begin to fade. To understand more of the mindset of these early Miracle Hill pioneers, I conducted a focus group with Vera, Mae and Mary Alice in 1993. Later I talked with Morris and Doreen Hallford. Let me share portions of their stories.

Mary Alice Waren, my mother, hereafter referred to as "Mom," came with my father Gerald Lehman, in June 1957, while Dad was a college student at Bob Jones University. Mom's introductory meal at the mission was chicken neck soup and cornbread. Asked to work for free, Mom and Dad lived in a dilapidated house on the mission's farm, the location that would later become Miracle Hill Children's Home. Only two of their five children had been born at that time: I was three years old, and Arlene was one. Mom and Dad worked for six months, before taking a brief leave for Dad to finish his bachelor's degree in ministerial studies. They returned to the farm in June 1958.

Mom cooked for the men living there on the farm. She had no

funds for personal items, but the mission purchased medicine needed by her children, and a doctor in Pickens provided free medical services. Mom and Dad began earning $5 per week in December 1957, a sum that had increased to $25 per week by 1962. With help from the mission's Board, Mom and Dad built a home in 1970, just off the campus of the Children's Home. Mom lived there until her death as she continued to work at the Children's Home.

Mae Harlow, "Miss Mae," was employed in June 1957, two years after graduating from Bob Jones University with a bachelor's degree in religion. She was asked to work for free, and the mission provided her with a room (shared with another employee). The bathroom was down the hall. She lived off savings of approximately $200, accumulated while working as a secretary after college. Her family was able to provide little financial help. She began earning a salary of $2.50 per week six months after beginning work, but by 1962, she was still making less than $20 per week. She acquired her first car in 1967 when the mission gave her a worn-out car to use as a down payment. Never married, Mae lives in a small home in Greenville.

Vera Wright, "Miss Vera," was employed in June 1958, upon graduation from Bob Jones University with a one-year secretarial certificate. She was asked to work for $10 per week, and the mission provided her with a shared room and use of a bath down the hall. (Mae was her early roommate.) By 1962, Vera was still making less than $20 per week. She acquired her first car, a used one, in 1972. It lasted 14 years. She never married. In June 1993 she moved out of ministry housing and began making payments on a small home.

Morris and Doreen Hallford worked at Miracle Hill from 1959 and 1960 respectively, until leaving in 1983. Morris began work as a single school teacher fresh out of college in 1959 for $10 per week. After college, Doreen taught for two years, a year in Maine and a year at Pensacola Christian School, before returning to South Carolina in 1960 to marry Morris and work at Miracle Hill Children's Home.

In January 1963, their oldest child was six months old, when the old farmhouse they were living in at the Children's Home campus burned during the Sunday morning service. I still remember someone interrupting the service to say the house was on fire. Their belongings were destroyed except a couch, a suitcase, a breadbox, and the bedding off their bed — which was all the teenage boys could grab before the fire grew too intense. The Children's Home supply of linens, stored in one end of the farmhouse was burned. The children's choir, with Doreen playing, kept their previous engagement to represent the ministry at a church in Simpsonville, South Carolina, that evening. They arrived to find that the church had been collecting linens for weeks for the Children's Home, replacing nearly all the linens that had been destroyed. A dress brought that day by another member of the staff and sandwiches brought by a neighbor lady made the day bearable. The Hallfords served on.

God gave them four children, and the Hallfords moved into an old, dilapidated farmhouse on the Children's Home campus. Morris added onto the house and improved it at his own expense in what spare time he could find. When no money was available, he scrounged used materials and straightened bent nails to use for construction.

Morris took over leadership of the Children's Home in the sixties and continued in that role through the balance of his tenure. Doreen provided primary leadership in the on-campus school for many years until stepping down to less strenuous duties while continuing to teach in 1980.

In the early years the day started with wake-up at 5:00 a.m., a live radio broadcast from the mission at 5:45 a.m., a full day of work, the 7:00 p.m. evening service, and evening office hours until at least 10:00 p.m. Everyone was expected to work on Saturday mornings. On most Sundays the Children's Home choir, accompanied by some of the staff, traveled across the Southeast representing the ministry.

I asked each of this group specifically, "Why did you start working at the mission, especially for such low wages?"

"I had a desire to serve the Lord," said Mae. As a student at Bob Jones University, she expected to go to the mission field in Haiti, but that door closed. "I wanted to minister to people. I joined the mission to work with homeless women and unwed mothers residing there and to work with the neighborhood Bible clubs. Money was never an object with me. I told the Lord early that I would never ask for anything for myself, that I would accept what He provided."

Before coming to Greenville, Mom and Dad Lehman would serve monthly at the Fort Wayne Rescue Mission. "As I saw the pitiful, needy men who came in to receive services, I said to myself, 'I hope the Lord doesn't call me into Rescue Mission work,'" said Mom. "When the farming position opened up with the mission, we saw it as a good opportunity to train for service in New Guinea. We never felt the freedom to leave after that. We didn't mind working for nothing. When we began receiving $5 per week, I thought, 'Oh goody, now I can buy some graham crackers for the children to eat as snacks at night!'"

As Vera, a regular volunteer, sat in her car in front of the mission in 1957 waiting to return to college when she felt the Lord call her to serve there, and she came to follow His will. "I wanted to work in an office, and I wanted to work with children," she said. "When I heard about an opening at the mission, I got to do both. Ten dollars a week was a sufficient salary for me. It was my first real job. Sometimes the mission bought me a bus ticket to visit my family in Michigan."

While still a college student, Morris wrote the *Saturday Evening Post* to protest their advertising policy when the magazine started taking advertisements for alcohol. He felt God ask, "If you feel so strongly about the dangers of alcohol, what are you going to do about it?" Morris gave up his Christmas vacation to fill in for one of the staff at the Children's Home, and he discovered that many were children of alcoholic parents. He came to serve at Miracle Hill full time upon college graduation with a salary of $10 per week.

"When I began working, there was nothing extra for working wives," said Doreen, "but we made it. Donated clothes for our family was such a help. I never bought a coat for anyone in the family until our second daughter, who was born in 1964, was twelve."

"The staff once went for twelve weeks in 1966 without a paycheck. Was that your worst time?" I asked.

"There was no worst time," said Mae. "The hardest time for me financially came when I moved out of the mission and began paying my own expenses."

Vera didn't remember any suffering. "We were all in the same boat, and our needs were being met. We never went without."

"Probably the worst time was in the early years when the only thing I could cook was what had been given recently," said Mom. "We had a lot of grits, cornbread, and eggs. Often the director would drive up with guests for breakfast. I would only know he was coming as he drove up the lane blowing his horn. I never knew how many people he would have with him or if I would have food enough for all of them."

When asked, "Did you ever think about leaving?" Mae replied,

"In my first eight years, I resigned three times and was fired once. I got discouraged working for Brother Tom. An hour after I was fired, Tom called me with a project he wanted me to do. When I refused, F. A. Lawton, a Board member, came to see me, encouraged me, and gave me some money to go shopping that afternoon. I reported back for work the next morning. Each time I quit, one of the Board members would encourage me to continue. They didn't promise me Tom would change. They just reminded me of the needs of the families we served."

I have never thought of quitting over money," Vera said thoughtfully. "I did get really discouraged once in 1983 when Morris and Doreen left. I called my mother in Michigan to tell her about it, and she said, 'So you're going to quit too?' I thought about it, and decided to stay."

My father considered quitting in 1970 during a time of real division among the staff. He thought about offering the Children's Home to another ministry. Mom told him, "We've come too far to quit now." Mom believed quitting would "make us feel like we'd failed."

"I'll take the bull by the horns and plow ahead," Dad responded. He never again talked about quitting.

Morris rephrased the question. "It was never a question of asking if I should stay. My approach was to say, 'Lord do you want me to go?' If I didn't hear an answer clearly, I knew I was to stay."

In response to the question, "Would you do it all over again?" each answered "Yes."

Vera was more forceful than that, "Mercy, yes! And I'm not even being spiritual. I have been able to serve in the ways I wanted to—office work and children. I have seen many lives changed. When children come back for reunions we can see how much has been accomplished. I would do it all over again. I wouldn't change a thing."

"A great motivator for me," said Mae, "has always been my fellow workers and the fellowship we share. Even though the successes are often few and far between, look at all the children that have been reached for the Lord. Yes, I would do it all over again."

"To survive those early years we had to be dependent completely on the Lord," said Mom. "I wouldn't trade those lessons for anything."

Speaking for the Hallfords, Doreen said, "We were a good fit there. We belonged. My most meaningful experience involved students who were there for quite a while. It was and is a thrill to see how they've changed and drawn close to the Lord."

With that spirit of sacrifice, is it any wonder God has shown Himself so mightily at Miracle Hill over the years?

❧ EIGHT ❧

Now, Do It Better

For many years in the history of our ministry we built what we could afford. Because we could afford little, we built facilities cheaply. Because they were low-cost at the time they were built, many of our buildings looked shoddy and were expensive to operate and to maintain. Yes, God had provided for Miracle Hill miraculously, allowing the ministry to grow larger than anyone had thought really possible, but our approach to improvement was self-defeating. With the backdrop of my business training, I knew not to spend money we didn't have. When we faced expansion, or planned a new building, I first asked, "What can we afford?" The answer was, of course, "very little." But as we planned modestly, we remained frustrated that we could never seem to improve our circumstances.

In August 1985, I asked Jim Cannon, at the time director of the Rescue Mission and one of our most effective staffers, to go to the Children's Home to assess our program and the physical plant. After looking things over thoroughly and interviewing members of the staff, he said, "If I were operating the Children's Home with the funds they are currently spending on operations, I'd leave behind your entire physical plant and start fresh somewhere else." Impossible dream!

The staff worked sacrificially, doing all they could with the resources available, but there were few resources available. The girls' dorm had only a few mirrors, there were none in the bedrooms of the teenage girls. And any mother of a teenage girl will tell you that was a real deprivation! Even irons and ironing boards were in short supply. The block buildings were clean but uninsulated and unattractive.

During this time as we planned ahead, (thankfully, before God provided the funds for the first new cottage) we changed the questions. Instead of asking, "What can we afford?" we asked, "If money were not a problem, what is the ideal solution for this need?"   That helped us develop a new sequence of steps:

- analyze the need
- gather with other committed Christians, staff and volunteers, who care about the need and will pray earnestly
- design the ideal solution to meet the need after seeking God's guidance
- figure what this ideal solution will cost and begin praying for God to provide for it
- use self-control, and instead of going into debt; wait until it is clear that God is providing funds

When we began to plan in this way, suddenly we discovered that money had never been the problem! The problem was a lack of faith and vision. If we wanted to work with homeless men, women, and children in cramped, inadequate, inefficient shelters, God was willing to let us do so. But when we began seeking Him in faith that He would provide what was really needed, He seemed delighted to help out in that way as well!

When God provided funding for the first cottage at Miracle Hill, we built with excellence. Then He began providing sequentially for other new or remodeled facilities until all of the children were housed in attractive, energy-efficient surroundings. By waiting until God clearly showed His supply, we were able to move into these new quarters debt free.

We were not out of God's will when we operated with our earlier mindset, but we were all much more encouraged operating under a new mindset. God tested our faith further, as we began planning for additional women's services downtown.

When the Greenville Rescue Mission began occupying its newly renovated quarters in 1973, there were 12 beds for women and 50 beds for homeless men—more than before, and more than enough to meet the need, at least for awhile. In the early 1980s the number of men and women coming to the mission began increasing by about ten percent per year. We added more bunk beds, even some around the back of the men's living room. To accommodate up to 90 men per night, men even slept on the living room couches.

The number of women and women with children increased. The upstairs had been a mixture of staff and women's quarters. By converting one of the staff apartments for use by the women, we were able to accommodate 22 women and children. Many nights every bed for women and children was filled.

We had always prided ourselves on not taking government funds. We had always heard that if you took government monies, you couldn't share the gospel, that you would give up spiritual control of the ministry. But I felt it necessary to discover if that were really true. The need to expand the Rescue Mission seemed like an ideal test case. After extensive discussions with the Greenville County Redevelopment Board, we found that they were willing to fund an addition onto the mission that would provide an expansion of approximately 60 beds to our existing facility.

We applied for, and received approval for, a grant of $200,000, to provide for this construction. This entire process occurred with full disclosure of the spiritual nature of our ministry, our religious services, Christian counselors, and active sharing of the gospel. The local Board making decisions on those grants was satisfied with all of that.

We completed the architectural work and went to sign the final papers for the transfer of the funds to Miracle Hill Ministries. Upon instructions from our Board, I asked once again, before we signed the papers, "Are there any limitations within this grant that would keep us from sharing the gospel?"

The answer was, "No, of course not."

Then the man added, "Wait. We have a new memo from Washington. Let's look at it together before I give you a final answer."

As he checked the memo, he found new regulations that at the time would not allow us to require religious services in the facility, would not permit religious verses or icons upon our walls, and seemed to imply we could not even enforce the strict life code that we asked our clients to follow. With deep regret and disappointment, we told them we would not accept the grant.

I was deeply puzzled by all this, because the mission clearly needed to expand. There seemed to be general agreement within our community that more beds for the homeless were needed. I feared that if we did not expand, a shelter funded by government might open without a spiritual focus. Although it wasn't essential that we provide the needed services, because the primary need of the homeless is spiritual rebirth and renewal, we wanted whoever provided the services to be evangelical Christian. But God had slammed the door on this government grant. We did not know how to begin a capital campaign, and we probably weren't mature enough as a ministry to begin one had we known how. For the next five years we waited while seeing conditions at the Mission become more and more crowded.

Finally, in 1990, we came to believe that we had reached a level of maturity and community support, so that we could raise funds privately to build additional capacity for the homeless. We began to realize why God had earlier shut the door. We realized that it would be better for the women and children in our care to be in a separate facility rather than in the same building with the men.

Many of the women who sought shelter with us came from backgrounds of immorality and/or abuse. Many of them, even though living in separate quarters, remained in fear because of harm done to them by men in the past. Though we had strict rules forbidding contact between men and women, inevitably some would find a way to make contact. Many of the women would arrange a meeting a few blocks away with men they met at our facility. They would then leave together and never return, reversing the progress they had made while in our care.

Though we did not realize it, many women who needed help would never approach us for it. I remember how vividly this was shown to me. As I left my car in the mission parking lot one morning during a downpour, I noticed a well-dressed woman of about 35 walking down the sidewalk toward the railway depot and the rougher section of town. With no umbrella or coat, she was drenched by the time she reached our parking lot. I intercepted her and asked her to come inside. I told her that we would help her dry off and take her to wherever she needed to go. She looked up at the sign and hesitated. I sensed immediately that she didn't want to be seen going into a "Rescue Mission." "If you come in," I promised, "we'll take you to a private back room. No one will see you or know that you are here."

She was more needy than I realized. An alcoholic, she had been fired from her job as a bank teller that morning. However, she would never have come to a Rescue Mission to get help.

She was simply walking mindlessly through the rain. She had no destination in mind, and no knowledge of where she was going. God used her and others to open our eyes to realize that there were many women out there who needed help — women who believed a "Rescue Mission" was only a place for the dregs of society.

As a result, we convened an advisory committee composed of Board members, donors, and friends from the community and began brainstorming around the need. As we began meeting and praying together we discovered that God had laid it upon the heart of a number of people at Christ Church (Episcopal) that another shelter was needed in town. As we began talking with them, they came to realize that we were serious about expansion. They offered their support and two men from their group, Jim Scott and Tom Sowden, joined to help our committee plan a capital campaign for a new women's shelter.

I initially thought we would need $250,000 to $300,000 to acquire or build a new women's facility. Perhaps we could buy the old Heart of Greenville Motel, a run-down hotel off Pendleton Street in Greenville. It was in a rough neighborhood, rife with drugs and crime. As you can tell, I was still suffering from a shortage of vision. With a focus on cost, I was prepared to suggest a place that no self-respecting woman would ever come for help and where few women would be brave enough to volunteer.

Tracy McAlister, a realtor and member of the capital campaign committee, recommended that we consider an empty office building just off North Pleasantburg Drive, near its intersection with Wade Hampton Boulevard. I was skeptical about locating in the heart of a business and residential district in a better section of town, but the committee liked the idea. The new location seemed affordable, and there was a bus stop nearby. There were entry-level job opportunities within walking distance at local restaurants and grocery stores. A nearby university could provide a ready source of volunteers. Someone observed that this might be the safest part of town. The university, located just across the street, had excellent security and even patrolled their fence at night. Our clients would be able to walk home from work after dark without fear. While it might make sense to locate a men's shelter within a needy neighborhood, most of the women who came to us for help were brought by someone who had transportation. We did not need to be in a rough section of town to serve women who might come from there.

Cost proved to be the next challenge. God seemed to support our choice of location, but this 20,000 square-foot building, which had first listed for $900,000, was on the market for $600,000. We thought we could scrape together a down payment. We offered a contract to purchase it at $400,000 with a $10,000 down payment and a commitment to pay off the balance within one year. The owner rejected our offer. I didn't know what to do, but knew by now that the building and the location seemed ideal.

But God had now given the vision to others. Four Christian businessmen, Lang Ligon, Tom Sowden, Larry Laplue, and Neb Cline, began talking together. "What if we came together as investors to purchase the building? We might have more leverage by offering cash. If Miracle Hill succeeds, we can sell them the building. If not, we can simply resell it to someone else later." In June 1991, their cash offer of $275,000 was promptly accepted. Fundraising for the new shelter began taking off, and before Christmas of that year Miracle Hill had purchased the building for itself. Each investor gave up any interest he might have earned and made an additional generous gift to the project.

If I had known the final cost in those first few months, I wouldn't have had faith that the new shelter would be possible.

But by the time we dedicated the building on February 14, 1993, God's valentine gift to the women of the Upstate, God had provided more than $900,000 in cash and in-kind gifts! The building was paid for as well as its renovation, furnishings, and some of the early cost of operations.

How did God put His lovely, special stamp of approval upon this new outreach? The very first night that women and children stayed in the building, a precious baby was born in the new facility! It wasn't in our grand design, but when the EMS arrived to take the mother to the hospital, they realized they had no time for that. Instead they delivered the child there at Shepherd's Gate. That squalling infant was our tangible evidence of God's grace and care for this ministry.

After the completion of Shepherd's Gate, the 22 mission beds formerly used for women and children were converted for use by men. The Rescue Mission was able to function adequately for a few more years. But by 1995, it became evident that more room would be needed for homeless men. We had conducted three capital campaigns in the space of ten years. Miracle Hill Children's Home had been rebuilt and a ministry to women had been established. A capital campaign in 1995-96 had funded renovation of a donated building for our Palmetto Boys Shelter. I wondered if the good people of Greenville would have any money left for yet another capital campaign to meet the needs of homeless men.

The mission building, then located at 571 West Washington Street, had been built more than 50 years previously as a city bus garage. Although its second story had been added when Miracle Hill acquired it in 1972, there were problems with the building that would be expensive to address. It needed new plumbing throughout, the heating system was failing, there was no air conditioning, a new roof would soon be required, and at 16,000 square feet, it was too small.

Once again we gathered together a group composed of a combination of Board members and friends from the community to work as a capital campaign committee. They began praying and surveying possible solutions. The committee looked at used buildings in other locations, but found none that seemed to fit.

When the property adjacent to the current building became available, it seemed best to build a new building there on Washington Street and tear down the old one. Although God had supplied a lot of money in the last ten years for capital improvements, I feared He might be running short.

So I was prepared to aim low. "What if we set a capital campaign target of $800,000 for the new Rescue Mission?" But while I had been talking theory that if money weren't the problem what would be the ideal solution, volunteers serving on the capital campaign committee seemed to be actually getting it. Someone said out loud, "If money were not the problem, what is the ideal solution for the needs of homeless men in Greenville?"

Tom Bennett, our CFO, came up with three possible solutions — –a minimal solution would cost $1,600,000, a more effective approach would cost $1,800,000, and the ideal solution would cost—hold your breath! —$2.2 million.

As we discussed which of the solutions we should pursue, we learned that other capital campaigns were being conducted in Greenville County at that time for an estimated $60,000,000. Perhaps this was not be the year we should attempt it.

Then someone asked, "What year do we think other people will stop raising money and make room for us to do so?"

Committee member Jane Derrick said, "If God is in this thing, He would want us do it right. Let's go for the whole enchilada!"

We continued to meet, pray, and invite people to participate in this new vision. Within two years of beginning the process, by the summer of 1997, we had received sufficient gifts and pledges to complete the $2.2 million project!

Tony McJunkin, head of our physical plant, had been going to contractor's school for several years. This, his first project upon receiving his contractor's license, was of greater magnitude than anything else we had ever done. We had challenges with the soil under the foundation, with scheduling the subcontractors, many of whom were donating a portion of their labor, with donated materials and with rising costs. There were architectural challenges, and we found it necessary to modify our plans as the building progressed. Nearly two years passed from the time we began construction until we occupied the new facility in the fall of 1999.

Because we were still completing the design as we went along, we didn't realize the final bill, $3.3 million, would be much greater than we originally estimated even with the donated services provided. Upon completion, nearly $1,000,000 was needed to pay for the building. Oh, the patience of Miracle Hill's Board! If I had been a Board member, I would have seriously questioned the competence of staff leadership during this process. Yet, the Board was patient and did not panic.

The Lord was so kind. Within nine months of moving in, gifts and pledges were in hand to pay off the final amount. God knew all along how much the new facility would cost. I think that though we had stretched our vision to get to $2.2 million, we did not have sufficient vision for what was really needed. This Rescue Mission building, which I envisioned raising perhaps $800,000 for, was worth more than $3.5 million, and God provided more than $3.3 million to build it!

We had made up our minds that if this project was worth doing, it was worth doing really well. This experience taught us one thing more: with our best wisdom, our most careful planning, our sincere caution, unless God Himself came to our aid, all else was useless. "Unless the LORD builds the house, its builders labor in vain" (Psalm 127:1).

NINE

The Beauty of God's Timing

In the spring of 1998, fundraising for the new Greenville Rescue Mission building on West Washington Street had been completed, and the mission was under construction. Our contributors in Greenville had given generously and had made adequate provision to serve the needs of the homeless. Funds for operations seemed to be adequate. We began asking the Lord if He wanted us to expand to meet the needs of the homeless elsewhere.

We heard that there was a need for additional shelter beds in the city of Spartanburg, 45 minutes away. Jill Evans, Miracle Hill's head of development, and I began meeting with leaders in Spartanburg to discover their perceptions. Many of the human service agencies believed there was a need they hoped Miracle Hill would fill. But many local churches believed that the Downtown Rescue Mission, already in existence, was doing a good job. Others felt it was only a Boarding house. "If you have a job and can pay rent," they said, "then they have an open bed. If you are homeless and unemployed, they are full."

It became clear to us that the only way we could begin a shelter in Spartanburg was to convince the community that the Downtown Rescue Mission did not deserve their support. I felt a great burden to help meet the need in Spartanburg, but I did not feel we could build the kingdom of God by vilifying another ministry. I deeply felt the need, but I also knew God did not want us purposely to create a division within His body. So, with reluctance, we decided the door was closed to ministering in Spartanburg.

A few months later the head of the Upstate Homeless Coalition, an organization supported by federal dollars that coordinates government subsidized programs for the homeless in 10 Upstate counties, asked us to consider opening a Spartanburg shelter. We explained the reasons we had already decided it was not feasible. "Then consider Cherokee County. Women and children often sleep in the woods because there is no safe refuge for them. If you come to Cherokee County, there will be fewer homeless people coming to Spartanburg to look for shelter."

Was this the opportunity we had asked God to open? When several churches and human service agencies in Cherokee County approached us about the need, we went to Gaffney to talk with them. We honored the lesson God had already taught us, that we must not allow money to hinder our vision. God wonderfully worked. In November 2000, Harbor of Hope, a 42–bed shelter for homeless men, women, and children opened its doors.

Then in the summer of 2000, the founders of Spartanburg's Downtown Rescue Mission called me. They were considering giving up the leadership of that ministry because of health problems. They invited Miracle Hill to take it over. But the approach they suggested, although reasonable from their point of view, presented serious ethical challenges. Again, I felt a real burden to help with ministry there, but knew we could not accept the offer.

Meanwhile, through the rest of 2000 and into 2001, Miracle Hill struggled financially. For more than a year, our cash flow for operations was negative, for several reasons. The stock market had sagged, we had lost experienced development personnel, and donations had not increased sufficiently to meet our higher operating expenses, no matter how hard we tried to raise support. Though we received gifts for facilities and for endowment, we lacked funds for daily operating needs. We had to operate programs with less staffing than client needs required. I became very weary of praying without seeing any answer!

That fall, evangelist Doug Whitley gave a vivid portrayal of the life of George Mueller in a service at Southside Fellowship, where I'm a member. Dressed in period costume, he spoke as if he were Mr. Mueller himself recounting the amazing ways that God had answered prayer for his orphanages a hundred years ago.[1] Doug recounted a dramatic answer to prayer and said, in an aside, "That would be more than a million dollars in your currency today."

I sat in the audience that day, and my eyes filled with tears. A million dollars? Why, Miracle Hill could catch up its obligations with half that! Why wouldn't God give us gifts the size He gave to George Mueller? I felt crushed and deeply frustrated that power like that was not available to us.

A few weeks later, as I looked at our cash flow and the year-end giving we could expect, I realized we couldn't possibly catch up by the end of the year. So I, with several members of our leadership staff, set aside a week to pray, fast, and to ask God to reveal Himself to us. Although the greatest need of the ministry seemed to be financial, we told God we wanted Him to work in our hearts in whatever way He desired. Did the Lord want us to close one of our programs? Did He want us to reduce staff further? That was impossible, we felt, without closing some programs. We asked God to reveal Himself and His will in whatever way He chose.

That Monday, as I prayed, I became convicted about the need for greater personal purity and consistency. I committed myself to it. I had been praying for rain for my friend, Bill Gressette's, pastures and hay fields and I continued praying. Later that day a donor raised the amount of his planned annuity with Miracle Hill from $70,000 to $101,000!

Tuesday, a woman who had taken offense at a stand I had taken four years previously called to say she was sorry and asked forgiveness. I was so glad to forgive her, knowing how much God had forgiven me, and I was especially glad for this evidence that God was working in my life.

Wednesday, I preached on fasting, and four members of the leadership team told me they too were fasting, some for the first time. At our leadership team meeting that morning, we made a difficult decision to change a policy on personal benefits for our staff. Since our wages were still low in comparison to other ministries, we had allowed staff to get extra groceries weekly from those donated to our grocery warehouse. God revealed that this might appear to be self-dealing or using resources unethically. We stopped this practice to ensure that our testimony in the community was above reproach, but we knew removing this benefit would be harmful to those who worked sacrificially with us.

Thursday, God sent the rain we had prayed for. A local foundation pledged a gift for operations of $10,000, another indication of God's working! That afternoon brought the death of a long time friend of the ministry, Mrs. Smith, who had been in declining health for several years. Also that day, I learned that I had hurt a former employee, and determined to make it right.

Friday, a Board member pledged $10,000 to help with the deficit.

From my journal for Saturday, December 1, 2001:

> *On Monday, I began a fast specifically to ask God to reveal Himself to me in power. The first few days, I did not spend much time with God—I was over-scheduled. But, the last few days, I have spent an hour or two daily. It has been puzzling because*

I have not felt Him speak dramatically. I have not felt especially close to Him. My reading today in Psalm 22 mirrored my emotions and my physical feelings so much. I've been feeling sorry for myself and very alone. But as I've also been reading about the persecuted church in Indonesia, I have come to realize that I want God to feel sorry for me, in comparison with my U.S. peers, not considering what is happening to other Christians all over the world.

We need $500,000 for the ministry to be current. This is more than we lacked last year, but even then we did not catch up. My dearest request would be to catch up and have a reserve by January. I confess asking God to be my "fall-back." I know He should be considered first, and I am asking Him to change my heart. I'm trying hard to be more open before Him. Lord, reveal Yourself to me.

On Sunday, I promised God I would meet with the estranged former staff member I had learned about on Thursday. I rejoiced with my friend Bill Gressette that God had sent rain for his pastures and hay fields as we had prayed. On Sunday afternoon at Mrs. Smith's funeral, I discovered that Miracle Hill would receive almost $400,000 from her estate, which would be settled in about twelve months. It was wonderful news to hear of that pending income. But it did nothing to help with our current needs.

By Monday, cash flow had improved, up to the amount we'd had that same date a year earlier. As we did an analysis of the past quarter, we found the number of Miracle Hill's active donors increased dramatically for the first time in three years. Bob, a former job applicant I could barely remember, stopped by to tell of a grudge that he had carried because we did not hire him. He told me that God had changed his heart and asked if we could be reconciled. Again, I was so glad that God was working in his heart and mine.

On Tuesday, December 4, a local foundation encouraged a request of $50,000 toward a planned new cottage for Miracle Hill Children's Home. I had not set a specific date for the ending of my fast, and I asked God, "Should I end my fast today?" I felt permission to begin eating, but not a clear mandate to do so. I tried to evaluate the previous week. We were excited about the pending Smith estate, but that money was still a year away. Although cash flow had improved by $65,000, we still needed almost $460,000 to be current. That was more than we could reasonably expect to gain in year-end giving. I had asked God all week if we should further cut the budget. Although I did not feel a definite sense of leading, I did feel a freedom to keep all our current programs open in spite of the deficit. God also gave Bruce Evashevski, our CFO, and other key staff peace about waiting on finances. If the purpose of the fast was to produce dramatic financial improvement, it had failed. If the fast was really what I had asked for, "to see God show Himself," it was a blessed spiritual experience.

While finances continued to improve during the month of December, as they usually do with year-end giving, we did not catch up financially. In January, after all year-end giving had been counted and cash flow was at its best in months, we still needed nearly $240,000 to be current. Since cash flow usually drops dramatically in the first half of each year, this level of need seemed irresponsible. We once again prayed and asked the Lord if we should make reductions. The answer, although certainly not a loud or clear one, seemed to be "wait."

Because growth in facilities and programs over the past three years had contributed to our financial needs, I assured our staff at our annual staff retreat in February that we would not plan to grow in 2002. We would stabilize what we currently had and build our existing base of support.

But, in February, the *Spartanburg Herald* began a series of articles raising ethical issues with Spartanburg's Downtown Rescue Mission that resulted in the resignation of its founders. The chairman of the mission's Board asked if Miracle Hill would take it over. As soon as I learned of the opportunity, my heart felt pulled once again toward a ministry in Spartanburg. Before that time, our inquiries had resulted in a door slammed shut. Now we had no need to voice judgment on another ministry. We had no ethical concerns about purchasing their ministry assets. Miracle Hill could simply assume an existing mortgage on the mission building and begin operations.

I enjoy challenges. Our staff members know to expect them, but this opportunity was frightening. This new facility and program would add $30,000 in monthly expenses. Prior to the newspaper articles, support for the Spartanburg mission had been adequate, but then giving declined dramatically and now averaged only $6,000 monthly.

Already, Miracle Hill needed several hundred thousand dollars to be current—much higher than normal for this time of year. In spite of that, we wondered if God was in this new challenge. If so, we needed to move forward on faith. Perhaps it was from God. Hadn't the burden we felt for Spartanburg continued, though we couldn't act on it in 1998 or in 2000? However, if this new opportunity was not from God, adding this new obligation could harm the entire ministry.

My wife Barbara urged me not to add more obligations. She knew Miracle Hill's financial needs, and she had seen my tears and my stress. "It's too much, Reid. You shouldn't add anything else."

A Miracle Hill Board meeting was scheduled for March 20 to make a decision. I knew that I had often accepted challenges that proved to be unwise. Accepting this one could mean I was putting Miracle Hill's other ministries at risk. Barbara was wise to challenge me, especially when I could not trust my own judgment about the decision. Once again I began to fast and pray, starting on March 12. I continued until Monday, March 18. This was an opportunity, though fraught with risk, that I deeply wanted to take. So I prayed, honoring my wife's wisdom, asking God to completely remove my will in this decision—to help me not to care which decision was made. To help discover God's will in the matter, I also asked that Miracle Hill's Board be unanimous in their decision—either for or against adding the Spartanburg ministry.

I spent a sweet week with the Lord. During the week, a local politician who had been angry at a stand I had taken three years earlier came to ask forgiveness. I saw spiritual victories in the lives of my family members. God impressed Barbara and me to make a yearlong personal financial commitment to help a struggling staff member. Others in staff leadership, although gravely concerned about finances, opened their hearts toward adding the new ministry. Barbara saw I was serious about seeking God's will concerning the Spartanburg decision. She withdrew her objections. God had answered part of my specific prayer: I truly had no will about the matter. I was at peace however the Lord directed.

In that difficult time we experienced a sweet indication of God's sense of humor. In 1998, after surveying Spartanburg regarding ministry, we asked community leaders in Laurens if they wanted to start a shelter. That door also had seemed to be closed. Now, as we were seeking God's will about Spartanburg, I had a call from Laurens County! The leaders of a small shelter work that had begun in the town of Clinton called to see if Miracle Hill would be willing to take it over. I declined, feeling that the current opportunity in Spartanburg was challenging enough. I suggested another ministry that might be able to help. But I found it humorous that God opened another closed door while we were seeking His will about Spartanburg.

At the beginning of the Board meeting to consider the Spartanburg proposal, it seemed clear that the Board would make the rational, responsible decision not to add additional operating expenses. I made no attempt to sway the decision. But as the discussion continued, our faith was stimulated by the godly viewpoints expressed and the commitment each member showed in seeking the will of God. Slowly, the perspective within the room began to change. By the time an hour and a half had passed, the Board sensed real unity that God was calling the ministry to move forward by faith—to add $30,000 in monthly operating costs. The Board voted unanimously to accept the challenge of ministry in Spartanburg!

On the day after the Board decision, the trust department of a local bank phoned to inform us that Miracle Hill was a beneficiary of a trust created in 1988. The death of Mrs. Smith in December (while we were praying and fasting) triggered distribution of this other trust. The trust paid out that May. Miracle Hill's portion, $829,000, was the largest single gift ever received by the ministry! The unexpected gift from this trust was enough to meet the cash flow needs that spring and to set a strong financial foundation for the balance of that year.

As we rejoiced in God's provision, I was reminded of my tears in that Sunday morning service the previous fall. "If God would do for me what he did for George Mueller, even if He provided only half a million dollars, I would know He cares about me!"

God proved He does care for me, and for the ministry that so burdened me! This tender gift from the Lord, planned years in advance, paid out as we completed a test in trusting Him. What an incredible encouragement to our staff — our decision, and God's immediate provision!

The Board discussion about Spartanburg had begun with the

practical reasons for declining the opportunity. It had ended with each member expressing a willingness to move forward by faith. Had the Board known of the pending trust prior to the meeting, the decision would have been easy. Instead, the Board stepped forward by faith and saw God answer immediately!

So we have learned, step by step, how to trust our God for the financial needs of this ministry He bears on His heart.

But God has taught us greater lessons. For what good are beautiful facilities, beds and food for those we serve, if God does not do His work in the hearts of the needy people we serve?

TEN

Lord, Give Us Just One!

As I returned to ministry at Miracle Hill in 1980, I wondered if and how God would supply my needs and the needs of the ministry. I didn't stop to consider whether He would change lives. I assumed He would, of course! For years I had heard my father and others talk about the success stories.

- the unwed mother who became a godly Christian wife to one of Miracle Hill's Board members
- newborn babies of unwed mothers who were placed in loving adoptive homes
- a man converted from alcoholism at the mission in the 50's who served there until his death thirty years later
- many older boys who came directly from jail to Miracle Hill Children's Home and had grown up to live successfully

I had heard these stories and believed that God could, and would, change lives. I had seen God supply Miracle Hills' financial needs, but I had not personally seen lives transformed, aided by any of my efforts. I assumed that transformed lives came from getting the formula right. If you take committed, godly, staff members, provide an alcohol- and drug-free facility, make strict rules, and preach the gospel, then you can expect people to give their hearts to God and give up destructive and sinful habits. Did I consciously think God was bound by a formula like that? No, but it was in my subconscious mind.

I certainly did not understand the miraculous nature of a life change. Generally people can't change. Certainly they cannot change themselves by mere will power. I know now that if someone experiences deliverance from sin and addiction, it is a miraculous work of God. Deliverance does not come from following the right formula. It is always a gracious gift of God.

Miracle Hill had a number of older, faithful staff when Barbara and I returned to the ministry. We began recruiting young couples, early-to-mid-twenties, to work with us. And with the arrogance of youth, we expected to change the world! Certainly we could bring God's power to bear upon the lives of those within our influence, couldn't we?

My first assignment was directing the Greenville Rescue Mission. My responsibilities soon expanded to coordinate all ministry operations. A friend from my lumberyard days, Wayne Scott, came to head our thrift store. Doug Van Scoy started as the mission night supervisor and soon became mission director. Dave Fuller came to head our maintenance, construction, and purchasing.

We instituted some early changes, saw good things happening within the work, and thought all of our efforts were focused to see changed lives through the power of God. Our primary area of influence with clients at that time was within the Rescue Mission.

It was quite sobering, at the end of that first year of ministry, to realize that not one of us could name a single individual served by the Rescue Mission in the past year, who seemed to be continuing in commitment to Christ. Dozens had made professions of faith before returning to alcoholism, drug addiction and other destructive, sinful behaviors. When we assessed the success of that first year of ministry, it was a tremendous blow to our egos and a real time of discouragement. Was the grace of God not sufficient for changing lives? Two thousand years of church history said lives could be changed by God's power.

But as I reflected on our failure to see others' lives changed, I came to realize I myself had some persistent, besetting sins. I found it hard to admit that I had major problems with the sins of anger, impatience, and pride. I had struggled with those problems for years. I had sometimes despaired of any hope of change in my own life, even when I wanted it desperately.

And, Barbara continued to struggle with habits I had intended to help her fix during our first year of marriage! (As if I could ever fix them, or should have even tried!) We were not successful in our private lives in overcoming temptation. So why should we expect God to change others' lives? Perhaps no one ever *really* changed. Maybe the changed lives that Dad often talked about were the rare exceptions, not the norm.

Was it a lack of spirituality, a lack of commitment that prevented us from drawing upon God's power for the needs of the people God sent to us to help? I did not think it was a lack of commitment. Why would any of us work for such low wages, unless we thought God had called us? We worked more hours than anyone in the secular field could reasonably expect. We worked actively at soul-winning and discipleship, and had regular morning prayer meetings throughout the year.

But lives weren't changing as we expected. By year-end we were praying, "Lord, would you just give us one? Lord, please give us just one person whose life is changed. Let us see Your power exhibited in him."

And how graciously our God answered that pathetic, heartfelt, prayer in the life of Bill Guin! He was just one of hundreds of men who passed through the mission that year.

Alcoholism had shaped Bill's childhood. His parents separated when he was five. He sold newspapers and shined shoes to help support his mother. But he lived on the wild side. He celebrated his twenty-first birthday in jail for safecracking. After he was released, he began drinking and partying, as if to make up for lost time. He moved to South Carolina, became a heavy-equipment operator, and met and married Rose, an attractive mother of four.

At first Rose partied every weekend with Bill. But as they had children together, she began focusing more on her role as a mother. By the time they had four children together, eight children in all, Rose committed herself to meeting her children's needs instead of her own. She challenged Bill to help her build a stable home. As his drinking became more destructive, she pled for change. More and more of his earnings went to alcohol. Finally, she gave him an ultimatum. "Bill, you have to choose. Will it be the children and me, or are you going to keep drinking?"

Bill really did care for his wife and children. But he couldn't stop drinking. Their lives continued in opposite directions. Rose accepted Christ, and she became a better mother and an exemplary woman.

At first Bill sent Rose money to help with expenses, but never enough. Then Bill's choices came at a faster pace. He chose alcohol over his career, his automobile, his health, and even his self-respect. Eventually, he began to ask Rose for money. She would give him some when she could spare it. Bill had visited the mission several times over the previous year for a meal or a night's lodging. But he seemed to feel no impetus, no longing to change.

One night Bill was in a bar drinking with friends with whom he was staying. After a drunken argument with them, he lost his place to stay. He slept under a bridge that night and used the last of his money the next day to buy a drink. But it couldn't meet the ache in his heart. He was sick and miserable. He called

Rose. Unselfishly, she came to see him and offered to buy him a meal, but he was too sick to eat anything.

He spent another night in the bushes, and called Rose again the next day. Rose, her mother, and their seventeen-year-old daughter went to see him again. His mother-in-law slipped him $2. "Bill, you are too fine a man to let a bottle destroy your life. Why don't you get things straightened out with the Lord?" Bill spent the money on cheap wine, but as he lay in the bushes that evening, her words haunted him.

In our time of defeat, when Wayne, Doug, Dave, and I were praying "Lord, give us just one," Bill Guin came back to the mission. No longer was he looking for a warm meal or a bed. His mother-in-law's kind words had challenged him. That afternoon in February 1981, Bill came to the lobby of the Rescue Mission and asked to speak to Doug Van Scoy, the mission director. "I'm tired of living out there on the streets," Bill told Doug, "I want to get right with God and get my life on track."

Bill smelled terrible. His clothes were stained. Normally someone as intoxicated as Bill would not be allowed in the men's bunkroom with the rest of the men. Doug was understandably concerned that Bill's perceived need for Christ would disappear when he found something else to drink.

"Bill, I'll tell you what," Doug said, "I'll make a place for you here at the mission, but let's wait another day to talk about Christ." Doug was as passionate as the rest of us were about wanting people to come to Christ. But he had talked to many intoxicated men who didn't remember the conversation the next day. Later, we acknowledged God's sense of humor when we realized we had postponed the salvation of the first serious convert that any of us would see!

Bill was serious, and he asked to see Doug again the next

afternoon. He was shaky, very shaky, but he was sober. "Doug, I want to get things right with God."

As he came to Christ, Bill instantly and dramatically changed. As far as we know, he never took another drink of alcohol. He was hungry to grow in his faith, and Doug happily discipled him. Bill couldn't read or write, but he could watch Bible preachers on television and listen to the Bible on tape. From the day of his salvation, Bill dedicated his life to seeking the Lord, serving the Lord, serving others, and rebuilding relationships with his children. Although Rose had remarried several years before, she rejoiced at the changes in his life.

Bill remained at the mission as a client for several months while being discipled. As he transitioned out of the mission, he became a mission thrift store employee, driving a truck to pick up donated goods.

Bill moved out of the mission into a Boarding house next door notorious for crime, drugs, and prostitution. With many opportunities to stumble, Bill continued to flourish in his Christian walk. The owner of the house was impressed and soon appointed him resident manager. In exchange for reduced rent for his own apartment, Bill collected rent, evicted the drug abusers, and began maintaining order. Within a few weeks he had created a haven for men transitioning out of the Rescue Mission who were serious about improving their lives. Alcohol and drugs were banned. People who wanted to live in irresponsible ways moved on, and rooms opened for those who were serious about personal growth. The house became more profitable for its owner. Bill used his role as manager for personal ministry until he moved out into his own place several years later.

Along the way, Bill became a close friend with Wayne Ballard, one of the volunteers who preached regularly at the mission. When Wayne felt called to begin a church, Bill partnered with him, giving generously of his time, energy, resources, and prayers to help establish Unity Baptist Church. He served there for many years.

In 1989 Unity Baptist Church gave a "father of the year" award to Bill Guin. He had been reconciled with each of his eight children and had taken special pains to invest in the lives of his children who were struggling. All of his children stood proudly with him on the platform of the church as he received that award.

Jim Cannon, another friend who discipled Bill, had a burden to start an inner-city church specializing in unchurched adults and families trapped by the effects of sin. Bill gladly joined him in establishing a church to reach the people he was most passionate about.

In 1984 Bill left Miracle Hill and went to work for Dixie Waste Paper, a company that purchased waste cardboard and newspaper from Miracle Hill. Bill started as a tractor-trailer driver. His common sense and ability to get things done led to his promotion as a foreman supervising all personnel outside of the office. He served there until his death of heart failure in 1991.

Bill was far more effective in dealing with men in the mission than were those of us on staff who had never known a life of alcoholism. Bill's entire life bore testimony to the grace of God and God's deliverance. He could say, "I know God can deliver you." Scores of men found hope for change in their lives after seeing what God had done for Bill.

While we were asking God for just one convert, he changed Bill's life in such a way that none of us could take credit for it! It was very clear that God put the desire for change in his heart, and then used his mother-in-law to bring him to conviction. You see, what God starts, He finishes! "Being confident of this, that he who began a good work in you will carry it on to completion until the day of Christ Jesus" (Philippians 1:6).

The transformation in Bill's life was accomplished by the power of God, who wants to finish His good work in all our hearts.

ELEVEN

From God Fighter to Fighter for God

As I read the New Testament, I'm struck by the variety of approaches Christ used in performing miracles. He healed many that were blind. In most cases, He simply spoke. Healing took place instantly, completely. Yet to some He gave sight in other ways. On two separate occasions, in Matthew chapters 9 and 20, He touched the blind eyes to give sight.

But the account in John 9 shows a longer process. Jesus spat on the ground, made a mud poultice, applied it to the eyes of the one who was blind, and sent him away to wash in the pool of Siloam. The healing occurred after the man washed his eyes in the pool probably several minutes after Jesus began the process.

I am particularly fascinated by the account in Mark 8:23–25.

> *He took the blind man by the hand and led him outside the village. When he had spit on the man's eyes and put his hands on him, Jesus asked, "Do you see anything?" He looked up and said, "I see people; they look like trees walking around." Once more Jesus put his hands on the man's eyes. Then his eyes were opened, his sight was restored, and he saw everything clearly.*

Colossians 1:16 tells us that by Jesus "all things were created: things in heaven and on earth." So it wasn't that Jesus didn't have the power to provide complete healing immediately, either in John 9 or in Mark 8. Rather, for His own purpose, perhaps to instruct us, He chose to heal in stages. After the miracle is recorded in John 9, Jesus uses blindness as a picture of sin: "If you were blind, you would not be guilty of sin; but now that you claim you can see, your guilt remains" (John 9:41).

Perhaps the variety of ways in which Christ healed the blind is meant to show that He uses many different paths to deliver sinners from spiritual bondage.

When we asked God for evidence of His staying power in a life, God gave us Bill Guin, the only spiritual evidence we could see from a year's work. Because of the depth of our need to make a difference, because of our discouragement, I think God specifically gave us a convert who was miraculously changed in just one step. It is the Bill Guins of this world who are featured on *Unshackled*, the Pacific Garden Mission's radio program. They make for dramatic testimonies. But what we had not been able to actually see was that God's miraculous work had already begun in the lives of others under the influence of the ministry. Most of those whom we have since seen delivered from spiritual bondage, especially addiction, have progressed in stages.

Yes, salvation comes at the point of specific decision. Salvation is immediate. "Whoever hears my word and believes him who sent me has eternal life and will not be condemned; he has crossed over from death to life" (John 5:24). But deliverance from addiction usually takes time. Many of those who had made professions of faith, only to go out drinking again a few weeks or months later were actually in the process of deliverance. We just did not recognize the signs.

In those early years, our programming for homeless men was primitive. Converts attended daily services at the mission, but there were no materials designed for spiritual growth to use with those who made decisions. Many of the staff worked one-on-one with individual clients to provide evangelism and discipleship. I normally met with one or two mission clients regularly in one-on-one weekly Bible studies that lasted months, until I felt each one was mature in his faith.

Few men at the Rescue Mission at this time would admit to a relationship with Christ. Others falsely claimed a relation with Christ, thinking they would receive greater physical benefits from the mission. To avoid judging the motives of clients, I sometimes found it wise to offer this personal Bible study whether a man seemed to be a believer or not. In 1981, soon after Bill Guin came to know Christ, Burris "Red" Owens checked into the mission. Red gave his name and some family information, but told us nothing of his background, nothing of the questions that troubled him. We did not pry. We've found, over years of ministry, that background doesn't matter nearly as much as what people do when they come into a nurturing environment and are given the chance to grow.

Red kept a low profile his first few weeks. Soon he was assigned to work the afternoon shift at the mission's front desk, answering the phone, and checking in new clients. I was looking for someone to disciple. Red seemed like an interesting, self-confident, intelligent guy. I felt drawn to invite him to study the Bible with me one-on-one. I explained that if he were willing we would meet for an hour each week to discuss a reading assignment from Scripture. With some hesitancy, he agreed.

We probably had the wrong guy in a public spot at the front desk. Red had been a brawler for years, as we later discovered. Good with his fists, he rarely lost a fight. Along the way he had lost the natural inhibitions that most of us have toward violence. While in his twenties he killed a man for mistreating Red's sister. Later, hitchhiking from South Carolina to North Dakota, he took the life of a man who tried to steal from him. His time in prison produced no visible benefits of repentance. What he wanted, he took. He did have a personal code of sorts. He explained, "I never killed anyone who didn't deserve it!"

Just before coming to the mission, Red accepted $200 and a 30/30 rifle as an advance payment for killing a man in West Greenville. Before dawn he concealed himself in the underbrush across from the man's house on Cedar Lane Road and waited. After daylight his intended victim emerged. Just as he began getting into his car, Red sighted in on the back of his head. But, instead of pulling the trigger, he thought, "If this is all a human life is worth, I may as well kill myself."

He did not carry out his assignment. The intended victim never knew how close he came to dying. Red took the gun and the money back to the man who had hired him. But then, he didn't know what to do next. He no longer wanted to continue his way of life. He didn't know how to change or what change to make. Frustrated, he decided that if he didn't find some answers soon, he would take his own life.

Not only was Red's conscience beginning to bother him, perhaps for the first time, but he was also experiencing his own midlife crisis. Years of hard living and heavy smoking had given him emphysema. Although he still won every fight, he knew his strength was waning, and it wouldn't be long until he lost a fight. Others would find out he was vulnerable. Red derived his self-esteem from his physical strength, knowing others feared him.

Although he would have said he feared nothing, he began to wonder what value he would have in the world when he could no longer solve problems with his fists. He knew he was feared and hated, but not respected.

Then Red remembered how much influence his brother had on those around him. Bobby, manager of a civic center in North Dakota, was known as a man of character, highly respected in his community. "When my brother walks down the street, everyone says, 'there goes a good man.' I want people to talk about me that way," he thought.

Red's heart's hunger to be respected brought him to the mission. He accepted an invitation from a 27-year-old, just over half his age, to begin a Bible study. In our first meeting, I gave him a reference Bible so he could search for the answers to his homework each week. He knew almost nothing about the Bible—every concept and principle we discussed was new to him. Near the end of that first session, I asked if he were a Christian. He answered quickly, "Oh, yes, I'm a Christian. I'm a Baptist. I've always been a Christian."

We began studying the book of Matthew. His homework consisted of studying the next few chapters and answering seven or eight questions that I had given him on the passages he was reading.

Red spent hours preparing for each session. He would look up the answers, check Old Testament references, and come back with questions of his own. About eight weeks after we began, he startled me by saying, "Since last week, I've asked Jesus into my heart. I've gotten saved."

Red began his new life as vigorously as he had lived the old one. Soon after coming to Christ, he was standing in front of the mission when a former client, very intoxicated, came by and soundly cursed the mission. Bystanders said that Red hit the offender so hard that he actually levitated horizontally two or three feet above the ground before falling! But Red's blow was so strong; the man's teeth penetrated Red's knuckles. His hand became infected with blood poisoning. The other man lost two or three teeth. Red ended up in the hospital.

"Red, I know you love the Lord, and you love the Mission," I pleaded. "God doesn't need us to defend Him. He can take care of Himself. Please don't hit anybody else."

At one of our weekly Bible studies, he waved a twenty–dollar bill he said he wanted to donate to the mission. "Now where did you get that?" I asked. "That's more than your allowance."

"I won this betting on football games last night. Now God has convicted me. He told me I'm not allowed to do that anymore. To clear my conscience, I want to give my winnings to Him."

We met weekly for two years, and Red grew rapidly in faith and its application. He became an outside employee, driving a truck for our thrift store. He began living in the Boarding house Bill Guin was managing beside the Mission. But his old habit called, and Red answered. That weekend he began drinking again. Consistent with Miracle Hill's policy, Red was terminated and asked to wait for a month before returning to the mission as a client.

Instead, when he sobered up, he went to stay in Greenville's Salvation Army shelter. Soon he began driving a truck for their thrift store. "Disappointment" is an understatement of the betrayal I felt. I was furious. I had seen others profess faith in Christ and return to an addictive life, and I was convinced Red was following the same path. I felt like I had wasted all of the time I had spent with him. (With today's insight, I wonder if my response indicated that I had been expecting some personal feeling of reward rather than simply giving my time to the Lord.) I concluded Red would spend his life moving from one homeless shelter to another. I felt his time with the Salvation Army was a retreat from God's call upon his life. Because I was so frustrated, I didn't call or visit with Red for awhile. My reticence, however, did not prevent God from working in his life; it just kept me from being able to rejoice in it!

Red continued to read his Bible and live out his new commitment. Many Wednesday nights, the church services at the Salvation Army included a Bible quiz. By now Red had studied the Gospels and the first six books of the Old Testament in depth, and he answered the quizzes well. Many of the other Salvation Army residents had a hard time reconciling Red's Bible knowledge with what they knew of his past reputation.

Back when Red had been working for Miracle Hill he noticed Rita, a young mother living at Green's Boarding House on Hampton Avenue. He often commented on how hard "that" woman had to work to be able to raise her two adolescent children. "She has a hard life," he would say. "Raising two children is difficult. I feel like I ought to help her out." When he moved to the Salvation Army he continued to help her out. After a while he asked her out. His admiration had turned into love for her!

One day he brought Rita a rose. "What are you doing next Wednesday?"

"Nothing special, I guess," she answered. "What do you have in mind?"

"How about we get married next Wednesday?"

She must have answered yes, because on a Wednesday in 1983, a clerk at Greenville City Hall married them!

Red's job with the Salvation Army was conditional upon his remaining a resident. So the night of his wedding, he stayed in the Salvation Army bunkroom. Three weeks later, Rita said, "If you are going to pretend you're not married, we can get this thing annulled."

Red went to the director of the Salvation Army, and said he was leaving to take another job. When pressed, he admitted that he was married and had kept it a secret. Instead of firing him, the director promoted him to warehouse manager, gave him a raise, and allowed him to live away from the shelter!

Rita managed their finances. Red provided stability and a steady hand. They saved enough money to purchase a lot with a mobile home on it near Marietta. Who would have guessed the fighter would turn into a married suburbanite?

Of course they faced challenges. Red's own daughter still carried the hurt of growing up without a father present. Now, this man who had modeled a bad living example for years was doing his best to help raise two teenagers. But he loved these children as he loved their mother.

Rita's daughter, Sally, moved out and began her own version of domestic life. When the father of her unborn child died unexpectedly with a heart attack, she moved back in with Red and Rita. On the day of the delivery the baby came so quickly that there was no time to secure medical assistance. Red helped deliver Sally's baby on the floor of their bathroom. With the arrival of Megan, Red was filled with a love he had never known before. When Sally moved out, Red and Rita began raising this newborn.

Sanctification is very much a work in progress. Although Red continued growing in Christ, he would occasionally spend a weekend drinking. These lapses frightened Rita. They would have cost Red his job had his supervisor known about it. Red's last drunk occurred one weekend when Megan was two months old. Rita gave him her ultimatum; "I won't expose Megan to this kind of life. If you ever drink again, don't plan on coming back. I'll just put your stuff out on the porch, and I'll raise Megan without you."

Red loved Rita and really wanted to live with her. But it was even more sobering to him to think of Megan growing up without him. Red never touched another drop of alcohol.

Red was rough, plainspoken. People knew he still considered physical force an option. Many who worked for him feared him. But he was a pushover to this little girl. Red delighted in his role as a parent/grandparent. There was a special bond between the two of them — stronger perhaps than any Red had known before.

As the warehouse manager of the Salvation Army, Red oversaw most of their thrift operations in Greenville. For years he supervised the efforts of staff and Salvation Army clients, producing hundreds of thousands of dollars in annual sales for that ministry. During these years his emphysema steadily progressed. By this time his leadership was more important than his physical strength. He continued to work, but he required a constant supply of oxygen.

In Megan's eighth year, Red's health became even more fragile. His physical decline continued, with multiple hospitalizations. Finally, Rita asked friends to take Megan for a few days so she could devote herself to care for him, keeping her promise to let him die at home. On the morning of July 16, 1998, Megan, more than 50 miles away, suddenly began crying hysterically, as if God had told her, without words, that her Daddy was dying. She phoned back to the house, and talked to the only father she'd ever known, just before he left this life and stepped into the presence of God.

When he died at the age of 64, Red had served with honor at the Salvation Army for fifteen years. His funeral was well attended by friends, former clients, and staff from Miracle Hill and Salvation Army. At his funeral I had to admit there had been a time when he didn't meet my expectations, but he was meeting God's.

I mentioned earlier that Red wanted respect: he had a hunger for people to think well of him. God gave him his desire.

Hundreds of men coming through the doors of the Salvation Army found work, hard-nosed accountability, and a call to change during Red's tenure. By his example many of them came to believe that they also could leave their former lives and follow the Lord.

Ironic as it sometimes seemed to me, Red would often say with tears and passion, "Why won't people do what they ought to do? Why won't they do what's right?"

Thank God, many learned to do just that, following the wonderful example Red had set for them.

TWELVE

From Burning Buildings to Building Buildings

If you want evidence of a life permanently changed by the Gospel, consider Leslie Kimbrel.

Les came from Bedford, Indiana, in February 1962, when he was 16. He had not planned to come to South Carolina, but it seemed to be a much better alternative than his current residence, the Bedford jail. Of course, he had never planned on jail, either!

His young life was rooted in bitterness. Born to a woman who eventually married six times, he experienced a string of broken relationships with the stepfathers who passed through her life in his first fourteen years. Most of them were alcoholics, or abusive, or both. He remembers at the age of seven when his mother determined to escape the abuser she lived with at that time. That afternoon, as he returned from school, she took his hand and began walking away. It was a long walk, and she didn't make it. Her husband caught them, took them back home, took all her clothes including the ones she was wearing and burned them so it would be harder for her to escape. His mother got at least one set of clothes, and escaped later by keeping Les out of school and leaving earlier in the day. Much of the time he lived with his grandmother and assorted relatives.

As he completed middle school, Les became very disappointed with his mother. She was totally involved with her new husband. "She didn't totally ignore me," he said, "but she was so deeply involved in her own life, I felt I was an inconvenience, just trailing along." Les felt neither close nor important. He was fed up with the turmoil, the turnover and the pain. He was tired of being afraid, of feeling insecure, of never having anything.

School, sometimes a refuge for children in difficult circumstances like his, only confirmed to Les that he was a failure. At his grandmother's request, the University of Indiana tested Les while he was still in elementary school. The diagnosis, in today's terms, was Attention Deficit Hyperactivity Disorder. All Les understood was that he couldn't learn like other children and his grandmother couldn't afford the special education he needed. His constant fear, and the insecurity of his home life, didn't help either. One year, while living with his mother, he attended seven different schools. "That year I was never at any school long enough to wear out a pencil," Les said.

He could barely read or write, and since nearly every subject involved reading, he felt there was no place in school for him to succeed. He disliked one teacher in particular. She resented having such a poor reader in her class. He resented having to sit in her classes. He avoided many opportunities in school because he was embarrassed that he couldn't read and knew other kids would laugh at him.

But even with its problems, school also brought hope: two shop classes. As soon as he started a class in drafting he knew he wanted to learn all he could about this subject. It appealed to his systems–oriented mind. There was a sense of structure. He had talent. He won an award with one of his drawings at the Indiana State Fair. General Shop helped as well. He loved working with his hands and won an award for a radio cabinet he built. His great aunt, who cared for him at that age, would read the shop books to him every evening. He would memorize the concepts and request oral testing in his shop classes. He passed these two subjects easily. He never missed a day of school.

Desperate to find self-esteem, he came to believe that money would help him feel better about himself. With lots of money he could buy clothing as good as anyone else in school. So he set out to get money for fine clothes, the best watch, a good radio, and the latest records.

Money was never a problem. He was industrious. He mowed 25 lawns; he was always picking up odd jobs. He had two newspaper routes. Actually, he was more "industrious" than anyone knew. He had learned how to break open the coin boxes in laundromats. The paper routes provided income, but they also served as a front, a way to maintain his image as a quiet, earnest young man, and a great excuse for being out before dawn.

One morning he thought he'd been caught for sure. With the money he had just stolen wrapped in newspaper in his paper bag, he passed a police officer. The officer took absolutely no notice of him. He seemed like such an unlikely suspect!

Les sought greater challenges. He began experimenting with explosives. Explosives led to fire. Setting fires became a form of payback. "People weren't hearing my cry for help." Les later said, "I was lost. I wanted to belong. Fires gave me a challenge. When I set fires, I was overcoming obstacles on my own." Les burned a storage building and a vacant house. He carefully planned and started fires on two railroad trestles. "Thankfully the fire department put them out before the trestles were too badly damaged," he now says. One newspaper article said, "These fires are the works of professionals."

Les prided himself on professionalism. But he made an uncharacteristic mistake. Since his great aunt was a hairdresser, she always had empty bottles around the house from her beauty salon. He used one of them to start a fire, but the bottle wasn't destroyed. Since a fire on a railroad was an attack on national transportation, the FBI was now involved. Patiently, federal and state agents worked their way through the supply chain until they got to Les. They arrested him at school.

"You are a failure!" Les accused himself. "You got caught. You're a failure." In his fear, shame, and humiliation, he began to pray for the first time. "God, if you're there, would you help me? I've made a real mess. Please give me one more chance. Just one more."

Les' aunt had taken him faithfully to her church, First Church of God. And God led two men of the church to get involved. A businessman, G. G. Johnson, took a special interest in Les. He began to visit him in jail. He taught Les about the God he had been praying to. Soon he led him to saving faith in Jesus Christ. From then on, Les' spiritual growth was remarkable. His fear of punishment was replaced by wonder at the love he felt from God and from his new friend. He came to believe that God had given him one more chance, that God would give him an opportunity outside of his prison cell.

Reverend John R. Butts, pastor of First Church of God, began looking for an alternative placement for Les. It seems miraculous, even today. Though Les was only sixteen, he could have been charged as an adult. His crimes had been costly to local businesses and insurance companies. In what Les believes was an act of God, the federal and state authorities turned his case over to the local courts. Upon urging from Pastor Butts, Mr. Johnson, and others, the judge allowed Les to choose his sentence: Indiana reform school or a place in South Carolina named Miracle Hill. Les knew nothing about Miracle Hill, but figured it had to be better than reform school.

How did Miracle Hill become an option? We think Victor Ashworth had something to do with it. Vic was a reformed alcoholic and an effective servant of the Lord, ministering to street people in Evansville, Indiana. In the early 1950s Vic had come to South Carolina to help the Greenville Rescue Mission get reestablished. Mr. Ashworth had followed the progress of the Greenville Rescue Mission with deep interest and had helped find volunteers to build the first building of the new Children's Home, Miracle Hall. He was thrilled with the continuation school there for older boys, and he began telling other Christian businessmen in southern Indiana about the school. Upon Vic's recommendation several other boys had already been sent to South Carolina.

Les was already committed to change by the time he arrived at Miracle Hill Children's Home. The bitterness was gone. He had a growing relationship with Christ. He was excited about this great, new opportunity. But he still faced challenges. He had never conformed much to the schedules of others, and his new school had rigid expectations for bed times, meal times, and classes. He had to give up smoking and the cuss words that had served him so well in Bedford!

But change comes easier when it's earnestly desired. The staff didn't have to give much instruction about the rules — the other boys took care of that. Leslie reports, "I knew I was in subjection." As best he could, he modeled his new faith in Christ, adopted a pleasant spirit, kept a cooperative attitude, and became active in the programs of the Children's Home.

The school's smaller classes and the teachers' provision of individual attention especially helped Les. Since the school used the Laubach method of reading, Les began learning phonics and began memorizing irregular words. This system worked for him. As he began to read, his confidence increased. He became a good friend with other students. Miracle Hill has always had a family atmosphere, but those older students, back then, in some ways became an independent family, not dependent on the staff.

I was only eight when Les came to Miracle Hill, but my father told me some of his story. I was a little in awe of him. How could someone who had done so much damage in Indiana be so nice in South Carolina? Les was one of the sweetest guys in the school!

All of the staff rejoiced that God had changed Les' heart, but everyone felt a little sad for him. Les dreamed of becoming an architect, but with his reading skills he was shooting for an unattainable goal. His goal at Miracle Hill was to complete school and go on to architectural school. But he had started so far behind! Could he even finish high school? But what Les lacked in educational foundation, he made up for in perseverance. He was doggedly determined to finish what he had started. Two years later, in April 1964, Les received his high school graduation certificate from Miracle Hill, and he was recognized as "best in citizenship" for the school. Who would have believed it back home in Indiana? The thief? The arsonist? Graduate with honor? Les had done well, but with his high school record, getting into college just wasn't a possibility, at least not yet.

After Les' graduation, a local architect, Avery Wood, took him in as an apprentice. Les next worked as a draftsman with the J. E. Sirrine architectural group of Greenville, and later for Daniel Construction. But from the talk of my father and other members of the staff, I realized no one really believed that Les could become an architect. They loved him and admired his determination, sure. But they didn't think determination could make up for his early educational deficiencies.

While traveling with the Miracle Hill Children's Home choir in 1963, Les met a fascinating girl at a service in Clio, Michigan. He saw her walk into the church and became interested. After the service as he waited by the car of the people he would stay with that night, she came out and got into the car. Although she was three years younger, Les was attracted by the fact that Linda was a strong Christian. They began corresponding, and in 1967 Linda became his wife. Soon after their marriage they moved to Michigan and later to Chicago as Les began working for the Wickes Corporation. There, Les and Linda raised their three children and faithfully attended a Bible-preaching church.

Along the way Les pursued his dream. He accepted every opportunity for continuing education. He took adult education classes in reading, study, literature, and strategic thinking. He studied technical courses at night, pursued one-day seminars, and volunteered for new assignments in the field he loved so much. Often, when there were classes he could not afford, he would persuade the teacher to let him sit in anyway. Although he didn't receive college credit, he gained the knowledge he was seeking. In 1992, twenty-eight years after Leslie began working in the field of architecture; he earned his license as a landscape architect!

Does God change lives? Well, Leslie Kimbrel knows that He does. Les's life verse is 2 Corinthians 5:17, *Therefore, if anyone is in Christ, he is a new creation; the old has gone, the new has come.*

"When I became a man in Christ," he says, paraphrasing 1 Corinthians 13:9, "I put away childish things. For me, childish things were harshness, cruelty, hurt, and pain." Les' passion, then and now, is to give glory to God for his healing and deliverance.

❧ THIRTEEN ❧

Healing a Broken Heart

As I mentioned, the changes in the lives of the people we serve are usually gradual. But let me tell you about Brenda Fowler, a woman who instantly and completely forsook her old life. We came to know Brenda in 1983 through a phone call from Bill Holland, a friend of the ministry who lived in nearby Spartanburg. He had given up his full time job to follow his special calling to minister to the needs of the street people in Spartanburg. Supported by several area churches and with some part time income from selling encyclopedias, he had opened Faith Baptist Church, a small mission church located in a twelve-by-sixty-foot storefront on Howard Street, which provided a launching pad for his outreach into that community.

Bill had become acquainted with Brenda as she staggered up and down Howard Street, intoxicated. In the early 80s on her way back from the bootlegger on Sunday mornings, Brenda often walked into his little mission church and stood at the back for a few minutes, listening to Bill's sermon. Then she would slip out again. For fifteen years she had lived in an alcoholic haze.

Repeatedly Bill tried to help her, but he knew that his words were not getting through to her. Sometimes she was too high on liquor to understand him. At other times, the temptations around her pulled stronger than the challenge of his words. How could she have come to this terrible dead-end in her life?

Brenda had always faced tough odds. Her father died when she was three; her mother died when she was eleven. After she was orphaned, her oldest brother tried to care for Brenda and their six other siblings, but Brenda was too headstrong for him to control. She dropped out of school in the seventh grade and never went back. She lived for two years with an uncle and aunt before moving back to her brother's at the age of sixteen. She began working in a cotton mill at seventeen. Although small, only 5' 2 ½" tall, she was athletic and attractive with brown hair and brown eyes. A year later she married Mickey Fowler. Within three years, they had two sons, Mitch, and Tony.

Brenda and Mickey lived together for five years. They had good times together, as they would have defined them: music and dancing, drinking together, and stealing together. "They were close buddies," Mitch said, "They could act so silly together. Mickey was Mamma's true love."

Brenda didn't even like the taste of hard liquor: her drink was beer. She drank on her days off—sometimes throughout the day. She drank a lot, but held down her job at the mill. "I was a good mother," she says. To his alcohol, Mickey added drugs, "speed," "uppers," and "downers." Brenda describes those days; "Sometimes he didn't know he was even in the world."

Violence permeated the home—but not toward the children. Mitch can never recall even one spanking by his mother and only one by his father. But often when Brenda returned from an absence, even if she had only been visiting her family, Mickey would be angry, and he would beat her. Mitch recalls one afternoon he spent fishing with his mother, her Aunt Geraldine, and his brother Tony. "I took Geraldine's cigarette case and threw it into the pond. Mamma jumped in after it. I kept throwing it in. She always found it." Brenda returned home, wet from her repeated dives, to face Mickey's wrath and a tire iron.

Although Mickey and Brenda were taking risks they could not afford, the boys fared reasonably well. They were neglected, but otherwise they were not abused. Mitch would sometimes wake up, frightened to find himself alone in the house, both parents gone. His Uncle Sonny and Aunt Geraldine lived just up the block, and he could always go up there, even if it meant risking crossing Howard Street alone. His mother and father might disappear for two or three days, but they would always drop the boys off with someone who could be trusted to care for them.

One day as the boys, now ages two and four, were away on a church outing, Brenda spent several hours at Geraldine's house, visiting and drinking. She had begun spending more time away from Mickey lately. He had been absent a lot, and was more out of control when angry. The boys returned home to an angry (and perhaps jealous) father. Soon after, Mickey phoned Geraldine. "Let me talk to Brenda . . . Brenda, your boys are gone. I called DSS and told them that you've been abusing them."

Brenda never learned what Mickey said to the Department of Social Services, but the cruel fact was that he had phoned them and almost carelessly relinquished custody of their children.

As you can understand, this was not simply a disagreement: in Brenda's grief-stricken mind Mickey had gone much too far. "How could he hurt the boys like this to get back at me?" she asked again and again. She had never liked the people at DSS since the days she'd been put in their care after her father and mother died. Now the DSS had her children, her very heart! Mickey could not have hurt her more. Brenda walked home from Geraldine's that day, with only one thing to say to a man who had betrayed her.

"Goodbye!" she said firmly. The argument quickly escalated to physical blows. Mickey hit her in the head, leaving a gash that required several stitches. As she struggled to open the deadbolt to flee the apartment, Mickey shot her three times in the back with a 25 automatic. Staggering, Brenda escaped and made it back to Geraldine's house before she collapsed.

Brenda nearly died from her wounds. Her recovery took months. The police pled with her to press charges against Mickey. But as is so often true with abused women, she loved Mickey, and she wanted to believe him when he came to the hospital to see her. "I am so sorry, Brenda. I'm sorry I sent the children away. And I'm very, very sorry I hurt you. If you'll give me another chance, we'll become a family again," he promised, perhaps too glibly. "We'll get our boys back. I'll quit using drugs. You'll see!"

Brenda forgave him, but all the time she was hospitalized, the boys remained under DSS care. In that time they never received a word from either parent. Finally, on the day Brenda was released from the hospital to return home, she discovered someone else had taken her place in Mickey's life.

Brenda used to drink because she liked to drink. Now, with physical pain and the emotional devastation of losing her husband and her sons, she began to drink seriously. She planned to get better and regain custody of her sons, but she had little education, a distrust of DSS, and didn't even know what accusations Mickey had made against her. She soon lost hope that she could reclaim her boys. She still didn't like the taste of liquor, but she began to drink anything she could get to ease the pain of losing her children. She started drinking as soon as she got up in the morning and drank until she passed out. Once she was given the opportunity to visit her sons, but the visit was canceled when she showed up drunk.

Life got worse. Her good intentions remained just intentions.

She came to a hearing for termination of her parental rights intoxicated. The judge saw her condition, and made the decision then to end her parental rights forever. Her sons grew up in a succession of foster homes and children's homes, always in the custody of the State of South Carolina. She gave up on ever seeing them again.

Sometimes Brenda was able to hold a textile job, sometimes not. No job lasted long. Occasionally she lived in a small apartment; more often with friends or family members. The one constant in her life was vodka. "I drank as much as I could," she said. Many of her drinking friends had money and held regular jobs. She often would drink a little less than those she drank with. She would wait until they passed out, and then leave with their money. She couldn't always remember what she had done to other people while she was drinking, so she often hid in her small apartment off Howard Street, afraid to go out, thinking someone might be waiting to "get" her. Every day she could get something to drink was another day that she didn't have to hurt or be afraid.

The law enforcement center knew her well. When she was convicted for public intoxication, she would serve four days in jail. After four convictions, she would be sentenced to four months in prison. But on her release, inevitably, she would start drinking again.

Her family gave up. The police gave up. The judges who passed sentence on her said she would never change. Everyone saw her as hopeless.

Everyone, that is, except Bill Holland. Bill believed the power of God could transform even Brenda's human heart from darkness to light: that He would forgive her sin and erase it through redemptive power of the blood of Jesus Christ.

So Bill Holland kept working with Brenda. Not even he

knew that for more than a year Brenda had been under deep conviction. Whenever she spent enough time in jail to get sober and think clearly, she knew God was speaking to her. But she didn't know what to do next.

One Friday Bill received a call for help. Brenda, calling from a pay phone, had just been beaten up. Before he could get to her, she was picked up by the police and jailed for public drunkenness. Bill went to the jail to check on her. She was in the drunk tank and scheduled to be released in four hours.

"I asked the director of the jail to hold her until she was sober so I could talk with her," Bill said. "Brenda couldn't be held longer without the court's intervention. We talked with a magistrate and pleaded that she be held until Monday morning. They agreed, and transferred her to the women's section of the city jail."

Bill was there to meet her upon her release on Monday morning. She looked at him with numbness and hunger.

"Brenda, Jesus loves you. He can set you free from alcohol and the life you're living. Wouldn't you like to ask Him to come into your heart and give you eternal life and freedom from all this? Brenda, have you had enough? Are you ready to experience all that you could ever want or need?"

"I'm ready," Brenda replied softly.

What an understatement! But that's the way Brenda talks. Sitting across the table from Bill, knowing she was held captive by satanic chains too hard for her to break alone, Brenda closed her eyes and received the Lord into her heart. She received the joy of forgiveness, and the hope of a changed life.

Since Spartanburg had no shelter, Bill phoned Nancy Lowe, then Women's Director at the Greenville Rescue Mission. "I need your help, Nancy."

So, that's the journey Brenda took to arrive at the Greenville Rescue Mission. Not only did she find a place that was alcohol-free, she found two new friends, Nancy Lowe, the women's supervisor, and Lydia Barnett, the women's night supervisor. Both began pouring their lives and their love into this needy woman. For more than a year, Lydia woke early every morning to meet with Brenda, at 5 o'clock, an hour-long Bible study. Nancy met regularly with her to encourage her. Immediately she began to assign Brenda tasks in the women's quarters. Soon she was appointed housekeeper of the women's quarters.

Today Brenda credits the power of God, the Bible study with Lydia, and the love she received from Nancy, with changing her life forever. She took her responsibilities soberly. She felt the deep respect and love from all of the staff, including my father, who approved the trust placed in her. All those around her believed she would keep the commitment she had made, knowing of the years she could not have kept a commitment, no matter how much she longed to do so. Now she acted with absolute reliability.

It is common that those saved from alcoholism relapse several times over several years before they find complete freedom. Brenda's response was uncommon. She never took another drink after she came to know Jesus Christ.

Barbara and I believed in her, too. For the next few years, Brenda was the primary babysitter for our two sons, Matt, four, and Andy, two. "I couldn't believe that you would trust me — me! of all people! — with your two most precious possessions," she says today. My sons love her dearly and think of her as their "second" mother.

At the time we made the decision to use her as a babysitter, we knew little of her background. We had no idea that God would use our two sons to begin to heal Brenda's broken heart. Our boys were the same ages as hers when they were taken from her fifteen years before. The older had dark hair, just like Mitch; the younger was blond and a daredevil, like Tony at that age. It was as if Brenda had received a second chance to love and nurture her boys. Brenda's broken mother–heart began to experience healing.

By the time Brenda came into the mission her children were nearly grown. Their formative years had been spent in foster care and children's homes. Her first priority, after she began to heal, was to reconnect and form a deep relationship with them. When he was 17 years old, Mitch received his first–ever letter from his mother. "I've gotten saved," she wrote. "I don't drink any more. I'd like to see you sometime." His social worker brought him to the mission for his first visit with his mother since he had been taken from her twelve years earlier.

She couldn't roll back the years of the clock, but her sons grew to love and respect her. She had always cared for their father. When he died, she helped them plan his funeral and supported her sons by her presence.

Brenda was promoted to become the women's night supervisor and held that very responsible position for five years. She stayed primarily in Greenville, fearful that she might be drawn back into her old way of life if she visited Spartanburg.

Then she felt God speaking to her. "It's time to go back." She began weekly visits to her family in Spartanburg, developing strong relationships with each family member. Some now know Christ because of her love and example. When there is sickness or death in the family, Brenda is the rock: family members look to her for comfort and encouragement.

In 1990 Brenda transferred from the mission to work in our

thrift stores, helping with the sale of donated goods to support the ministry. After living and working in Greenville for years, she transferred to Miracle Hill's Spartanburg store to be closer to her family.

Frank, the longtime bootlegger who supplied Brenda with Sunday liquor for years, heard she had changed. When she first began visiting Spartanburg again, he saw for himself the transformed life of the woman he'd enabled in her drinking. "It isn't what I've done, Frank. It's Jesus. Why don't you trust Him, too?"

Then Frank was diagnosed with colon cancer. At Brenda's encouragement, he entrusted his heart to the Lord. He died a week later. The hopeless drunk had led the hopeless bootlegger into the joy of eternal life in Christ!

⚘ FOURTEEN ⚘

Looking for God Every Day

Throughout the book I have talked about unusual ways and critical times in which God has shown Himself. But it is gratifying, also, to see God's hand in "ordinary" times of the Christian life. Wouldn't it be nice, even if there is no crisis, or, at least none that we are aware of, to see Him graciously show Himself and to know that we have been used by Him?

Many times we fail to acknowledge God's deliverance, especially in what might be called the "smaller issues" of life. We pass off unexpected, even miraculous, changes that occur in our lives as happenstance or self-discipline rather than the work of the Lord. While we still receive the benefit of the change that has taken place, we lose the blessing of seeing our faith strengthened and we cheat God out of glory by not acknowledging and praising Him.

Some seem to see God more often than the rest of us in the daily circumstances of life. Bill "Billy" Odom stands out as extra attentive. In 1993 Bill and Pat Odom came to Miracle Hill Ministries after serving with another Children's Home for more than 23 years. Bill and Pat seemed to see God at work everywhere. Bill looked for God in every daily activity, and he was always eager to share a story of what God had done recently. His excitement and love for the Lord were contagious. Often, after a conversation with Bill, I would leave feeling slightly ashamed that I was not pursuing the Lord passionately.

Bill oversaw Miracle Hill's development of a central storage area for donated groceries and personal supplies. In addition to supplying food for Miracle Hill's ministry centers, that warehouse provides groceries to needy families, and, when available, shares with other ministries. Bill served as head of that food warehouse until God took him home in 2002.

In his role as warehouse manager Bill refined a concept he called "sharing." Previously, when the ministry received a large in-kind gift, such as chicken or cornmeal, we would save as much as could be used that year, giving away only what would spoil before we could use it. Using the biblical concept, "freely you have received, freely give," from Matthew 10:8, Bill began giving away supplies. He would hold only enough to meet a few weeks' needs at Miracle Hill and give away the rest. When he interacted with other ministries he didn't trade tit-for-tat. He shared freely. Those other ministries had no obligation to reciprocate. If they chose to share their excess, Bill would take some for Miracle Hill and pass on the rest to other nonprofit organizations.

Every time I saw Bill he would share with excitement a fresh story of an act of God: sometimes in changing him, sometimes providing for Miracle Hill's needs, and sometimes in seeing Miracle Hill used by God to provide for the needs of others.

"Blessed is the man who listens to me, watching daily at my doors, waiting at my doorway." Although Proverbs 8:34 refers to the pursuit of wisdom, it also applies to a pursuit of the author of wisdom, God. Several scriptures in Proverbs reveal wisdom as the personification of Jesus. Bill lived that way every day, looking for God. And, I believe that when someone like Bill is so constantly attentive, God tends to show Himself more often than to those of us who are distracted by the pace of daily living.

One of Bill's favorite glimpses of God's provision involved

a family counselor at Miracle Hill Children's Home, Jane Pulido. In spring 1997, Jane had been working extensively with Tammy, a single mom with two teenaged boys. Tammy, whose boys had stayed for a time at Miracle Hill Children's Home, had begun a personal relationship with Christ, given up alcohol and drugs, found work, and was now mothering her sons to the best of her ability. In addition to her counseling, Jane had been conducting a Bible study with Tammy on the subject "Trusting the Lord." Tammy wanted to trust the Lord, but she was so frustrated.

"Why is it always so hard?" Tammy said. "Why can't I have what I need? I do believe the Lord will provide, but why is it always a such a struggle?"

Tammy was growing rapidly in faith, and she had recently made the decision to accept a niece into her home to insure that she received better care. At the time of her meeting with Jane she had done everything right. She had not wasted any of her money. She had paid the most critical bills. But on this particular day, she was out of money and had no food for her family.

As Tammy expressed her frustration, Jane challenged her to trust God. "Give me a list of the groceries you need," Jane said, "I'll go to Miracle Hill's grocery warehouse and see what I can find there. I think you'll see that God will supply your needs as He has promised to do."

Tammy provided a grocery list of fifteen items. Some needs were generic such as toothbrushes. For others, she specified brand: Red Band flour and Luzianne tea. As Jane came to the warehouse to look for those items, she was a little concerned because Tammy had been so specific. While there was usually flour, who knew if it would be the "Red Band" brand? Having tea available at all was less common, much less the Luzianne brand.

"Dear God, Tammy really needs to see your power and your provision right now," Jane prayed. "Would you be merciful and let me get each item on this list she has given me?"

The first few minutes of shopping were exciting. Jane found not only the items requested, but the exact brands that had been specified! For some of the vegetables listed, there was exactly the number of cans on the shelves that Tammy had asked for! Within about fifteen minutes, Jane had found fourteen out of the fifteen items on the list. But, there were no toothbrushes. That was a little surprising because toothbrushes were usually available.

Bill noticed Jane looking a little puzzled and came over to see if he could help.

"Bill, do you have any toothbrushes?"

"No, we're out at the moment," he replied.

"I'm trying to show one of the women I'm helping that God will supply her needs. I asked God for everything on this list, but I'm short on that one item."

"Look at the bright side," said Bill. "You've found all but one."

"No, I asked God for every item on the list today to show Tammy that He answers prayer."

As they talked, a staff member from a boys' home south of Greenville arrived to pick up groceries that we were sharing with them. Walking in he said, "We have extra toothbrushes at our place and I brought some along. Can you use them?"

"Can we use them? That's exactly what we're praying for!" Jane joyfully loaded Tammy's groceries in her car. That day God gave Tammy every single item she needed—brand specific.

One of my favorite memories of God at work in that ministry department occurred just a few months before Jane saw her special prayer answered. About mid-afternoon on New Year's Eve 1996, I had completed my work in the office. On my way home I planned to visit a needy mom with a mentally challenged, pre-teen son. Although the primary purpose of my visit was encouragement, I knew that this mom, whom I'll call Beth, struggled to make ends meet. So I stopped by Miracle Hill's food warehouse to pick up a box of groceries to take to her.

At the warehouse Bill was hard at work. But, he had time, as always, to share his latest story. That morning he received one of the rarest of all donated commodities, a pallet of fresh orange juice. He had eagerly called all of Miracle Hill's ministry centers, and everyone was rejoicing at this new gift. Since there was more than we could use quickly, Bill had called to share with "Detox," a local agency that specializes in taking alcoholics and drug addicts through the initial stages of sobriety.

As you can imagine, orange juice was an important tool in their program—their residents consumed gallons of it weekly. They had just run out of juice and realized that on New Year's Eve they would not be able to get a delivery from their regular supplier. They faced the possibility of going without for several days. Although "Detox" is a secular agency, they saw Bill's call as providential, and picked up nearly all the orange juice we had left.

"Just look at how God timed that gift and their need," Bill exclaimed. "Isn't God good?"

"He sure is!" I replied, and began filling an empty banana box with groceries for Beth and her family. In addition to normal staples such as flour, canned vegetables, cereal and crackers, I put in a gallon of orange juice. We virtually never have donated ice cream, but on this particular day we had received a pallet of first-quality ice cream. Pushing aside some of the commodities, I buried half a gallon of vanilla ice cream in the bottom of the box.

As I drove away from the food warehouse, I felt a little jealous. It seemed that Bill got to see God's hand almost daily, certainly more than I did.

"Lord, I wish that You would reveal yourself more to me in that way," I thought. "I wish that I could see your hand in my surroundings more often."

When I arrived at Beth's house she and her son were home. Her eyes brightened, and she seemed so glad to see me. I enjoyed every visit with her—I knew no one with more faith. And, she was grateful to receive the groceries, especially the orange juice. But when I pulled out the ice cream, she began to cry. "Beth, what's wrong?" I asked. "Why are you crying?"

"I was in the grocery store today buying groceries. Jonathan loves ice cream, and I picked up a box this morning. After the cashier rang things up, I realized that I didn't have enough money to pay for everything. With a heavy heart, I put the ice cream back. I left the ice cream at the grocery store this morning, and God had it delivered to me this afternoon. Isn't He good to us!"

Now, I had tears in my eyes; I had a silly grin—one that remained on my face all the way home. It wasn't just Bill that God was using that day. It feels so good to be used of God to meet the need of others.

God is at work all around me every day. So often I'm pre-occupied and fail to see His hand. I believe He reveals Himself the most to those who look most diligently for Him.

FIFTEEN

What's the Difference?

Many Christian ministries seem to be able to serve effectively for years without seeing extraordinary demonstrations of God's power. I'm not putting them down. Many Christian outreaches are biblically true, and evangelically strong led by godly, sincere people. Yet they record few striking interventions from God. What has been the difference at Miracle Hill?

I don't know all of the answers to that question, but I have a few ideas. And, please don't take my ideas as a recipe for pulling down the power of God. My ideas are simply my attempt to make sense for myself of God's wondrous provision here in South Carolina. He is God, and He may take quite a different approach with you.

There is danger here, as in any account of ways in which God has worked. One can easily fall into the trap of trying to place God in a box: to determine a formula by which we think God must act for us, a certain "right order" magic. While I have shared what He did in our hearts as He revealed Himself in this ministry, I freely acknowledge that He is God. He can show Himself, or not, in any circumstances and under any conditions He chooses. Our role is to walk humbly before him and to seek him faithfully. I can give you no formulas that will make Him act on your behalf. Better than any insight I can share, we both have access to Scripture, which shares His heart.

First, ministry to the poor is a cause God cares about. In the Scripture God tells us that the needs of the poor, widows, and orphans are especially close to His heart. Throughout the Old Testament God's people are told to help those in need in addition to giving tithes to the temple. More than 250 Old Testament verses refer to the poor, widows and fatherless. The New Testament reinforces our necessity to provide for those in need — Acts, 1 & 2 Corinthians, Galatians, and James. Someone who is "poor" is not defined in Scripture as someone with less money. The poor are those in bondage, oppressed, trapped in a situation they cannot escape.

The New Testament word most often translated "poor" comes from a root meaning, "to crouch." It was common at the time of Christ to see camels crouching, or kneeling, to receive the loads they would carry. One who is poor can be compared to a camel that has received too heavy a load while on its knees. The camel cannot get up, and there is nothing it can do to change its circumstances. The camel will eventually die, trapped there, unless someone intervenes.

Although Paul's first epistle to Timothy defines certain widows as being more appropriate for permanent church support, the Bible generally doesn't differentiate between the "worthy" and the "unworthy" poor. "If their circumstances are not their fault, I'll help," an opinion held by many believers, is an unscriptural qualification. Matthew 25:35 tells us our compassion for "one of the least of these" is a direct act of care for Jesus Christ. Some may be sick or hungry through no fault of their own. Rarely will those in prison be there in innocence. Regardless of who is at fault, the poor are trapped in circumstances inadequate for the care of body and spirit, and will live in misery, or even die in it, unless someone intervenes.

So, while God works visibly in the hearts of all who have personal relationships with Christ, a ministry to the homeless, such as Miracle Hill Ministries, is especially fertile ground for seeing Him at work.

Second, the ministry has attempted to ameliorate more human suffering than we've had resources or human strength to accomplish. Those attempts have not been with the idea of building monuments – either in buildings or in programs. We have simply tried to intercede with God on behalf of others who are desperately in need. Is it so hard to conceive, "The need is huge and we are small, but if we can touch the hand of God with our intercession, let's hold on and see what happens?"

In Luke 11:5-6 we read, "Then He [Christ] said to them, Suppose one of you has a friend, and he goes to him at midnight and says, 'Friend, lend me three loaves of bread, because a friend of mine on a journey has come to me, and I have nothing to set before him.'" With these words, Christ charges us to bring to God those we care about but cannot help personally.

The person we're asking for must be our friend. The same Greek word, *philos*, is used both for the friend we care about and for the friend whose help we are seeking. We must care about and reach out to the one in need before we can expect to ask God to respond to our request.

But in a ministry like Miracle Hill, the need is greater than we can provide. We should use our own resources if we can. The petitioner in this case could honestly say, "I have nothing to set before him." Finally, we must be willing to continue interceding on behalf of our friend. Going to seek help at midnight seems to indicate perseverance and a willingness to be inconvenienced.

Through the years at Miracle Hill, our staff have encountered such massive, hopeless human needs, that we could not effect any beneficial changes outside of God's intervention. Coming to God in this manner, our God's servants here have been able to claim verses 9 and 10, "So I say to you: 'Ask and it will be given to you; seek and you will find; knock and the door will be opened to you. For everyone who asks receives; he who seeks finds; and to him who knocks, the door will be opened.'"

Third, those who have served in this ministry have possessed an extraordinary spirit of self-sacrifice. I mentioned Jane Pulido. How can any servant of God ask with the confidence Jane used as she sought to meet Tammy's needs? The ministry of Miracle Hill has been blessed with many such extraordinary people through the years. I'm not sure our people have been smarter than other Christian servants. They surely have not been better trained or better connected with funding sources. Rather, the most striking characteristic of those who have served at Miracle Hill over time has been their spirit of self-sacrifice. So many of those who have served at Miracle Hill over time have cared so much about seeing God provide for the ministry, and about seeing God change hearts, their own personal needs seemed to matter little. Those who cared much about their personal needs and being sure their needs were met first seemed to get frustrated at Miracle Hill, and they quickly moved on to other pursuits. Those who truly put first the kingdom of God and His righteousness seemed to stay on.

Surrender in the area of financial needs has been critical. Forgive another reference to George Mueller, but my heart was so encouraged to learn that when things got really tight for the orphanages, he and his wife sold some of their furniture to provide for the needs of ministry. Was their action a lack of faith that God would provide? I think rather it was a willing offering, "God, I'll give all I possibly can. I'm not holding anything back from you. It's up to you to do the rest."

If you would like to see God provide for the needs of the ministry to which He has called you, can you afford to hold onto your own resources? In almost every case when we've seen God answer financial needs miraculously, the staff, in addition to fervent prayer, have personally given their own scarce resources. Several times in the past few years I've spent a week or more praying and fasting for Miracle Hill's finances. In almost every case I've felt led to forgo my salary that week, even if I have to use savings to meet that week's personal obligations. Earlier I talked about the sacrifices of those early pioneers. Countless sacrifices made here at Miracle Hill have been known only to God.

Fourth, those who have served most effectively have lived what they taught in a spirit of transparency. Now, those who have served at Miracle Hill had warts and sinful tendencies just as all others who claim the name of Christ. We've sometime had to ask staff to leave because of inappropriate behavior. While God calls us to purity, putting God and His kingdom first is not an absence of sin, but rather a continual daily focus on putting God's interests ahead of one's own.

The people we serve at Miracle Hill have real problems — massive, unsolvable problems. Pious platitudes just won't do. Quoting Scripture at them, even though it's the tool God uses to change lives, isn't enough either. When we want to see the lives of others transformed, we cannot hold anything back in our own life — secret sins, past hurts, or running from an issue we have never been willing to face. Some counselors have left our ministry defeated because there were issues in their own lives they were unable, or unwilling, to allow God to change.

All of us are broken in some way. If we're allowing God to continue His painful work of change within us, if we are willing to admit we're struggling, we can still help others change. If we deny we have problems, or hide our struggles, how can we tell others God can transform and change their lives? And so we have persevered in prayer until God showed Himself.

In many of those attempts, if God had not shown Himself, the ministry needs at that moment would have been impossible. There may be a fine line between tempting God and proving Him, but it's a line worth exploring. It would have been a foolish and sinful risk for Christ to throw Himself off the temple to see if the angels would catch Him when He was being tempted by Satan. However, Elijah took an incredible but godly risk when he called for fire to come down from heaven and devour the sacrifice on Mount Carmel (1 Kings 18). Had the fire not come, Ahab and Jezebel who had been looking for him, would have quickly executed Elijah. But Elijah, walking in obedience and in the power of the Spirit, called for God's power to be displayed for a cause close to God's heart, to challenge a backslidden nation on God's behalf. And, God answered.

May you find God as you look for Him, and may you also find yourself greatly used by Him as you surrender yourself to His calling for your life.

❧ PHOTO GALLERY ❧

Clinton Cottage
built in 1986
with help from
a gift by
Frank Clinton

Gerald Lehman
early 1960's

Algie Sutton (seated center)
signs check for $100,000 --
others from left: Jesse Helms,
Gerald Lehman, F.A. Lawton

Reid and Barbara Lehman
August 1, 1975
Doesn't she look young?

After the fire we started again with the concrete slab

After the fire -- the beautiful home God gave us

Matt and Reid as they begin their "homeless" trek

Andy and Reid as they return from living "homeless" in Savannah

Children's Home, located in Greenville in 1958

First school at Miracle Hill Children's Home -- a converted corn crib

Concrete roof trusses being delivered for Miracle Hall construction

Volunteers working at Miracle Hall, the first building at Miracle Hill Children's Home (1959)

Miracle Hall completed

Mary Alice, Gerald, Reid, Arlene and family friend in front of their first home at Miracle Hill Children's Home

Greenville Rescue Mission building 1950-1972

Greenville Rescue Mission building 1973-1999

Shepherd's Gate
building
1993 -- present

Greenville Rescue
Mission building
1999 -- present

Miracle Hill
Rescue Mission,
Spartanburg
building 2002

Bill Guin (left)
and friend
1982

Burris "Red" Owens

Brenda Fowler
and
Andy Lehman

Bill Odom (right)
helps pack food
boxes in the grocery
warehouse

❧ APPENDIX ❧

A Brief History of Miracle Hill Ministries

This ministry was organized in the fall of 1937 by a group of
Greenville Christian lay persons who were concerned about
the homeless and transient population in the Upstate area of
South Carolina. Two key early volunteer leaders were Dr. Paul
Beacham, president of Holmes Bible College, and attorney
John Henry, a strong lay leader in Buncombe Street United
Methodist Church.

The first known location was a building at the corner of
Buncombe and Laurens Streets across from Buncombe Street
Methodist Church. The location was known as Gospel Rescue
Mission.

In the late 1940s the work had grown to incorporate care for
unwed mothers and housing for transients in a larger building
at 1001 West Washington Street near the Southern Railway
Train Depot in Greenville.

A short history of Miracle Hill Ministries follows.

Date	Event	Annual Budget	Total Capacity
1937	opened soup kitchen on Laurens Street (the Bank of America Tower is currently located there)		
1940's	opened a small men's shelter: Greenville Rescue Mission (unwed mothers cared for)		
1950's	began caring for women with children in the men's shelter	$35,000	
1958	established Miracle Hill Children's Home		
1958	opened Miracle Hill's first thrift store	$133,664	
1973	Greenville Rescue Mission moved to newly renovated building	$156,000	
1985	Miracle Hill Children's Home changed to cottage style care	$681,400	134
1990	opened Palmetto Boys Shelter; board approves name change to Miracle Hill Ministries, Inc.	1,297,997	170
1993	opened Shepherd's Gate	2,114,922	216
1995	foster care program began; acquired Relief Ministry	2,747,926	225
1996	Palmetto Boys Shelter moved to new location	3,334,615	240
1999	Greenville Rescue Mission moved into new building	4,258,412	294
2000	opened Mission in Gaffney	4,148,065	338
2002	acquired Mission in Spartanburg	5,888,851	422
2005	names of Miracle Hill facilities standardized	6,500,000	422

Miracle Hill Ministries Today

- Miracle Hill Boys' Shelter, Greenville, SC capacity 18 boys

- Miracle Hill Children's Home, Pickens, SC, capacity 60 children

- Miracle Hill Relief Ministry, capacity to provide 430 families monthly with groceries.

- Miracle Hill Greenville Rescue Mission, Greenville, SC, capacity 160 men and five families

- Miracle Hill Rescue Mission • Cherokee County, Gaffney, SC, capacity 20 men, 22 women and children

- Miracle Hill Rescue Mission • Spartanburg, Spartanburg, SC, capacity 50 men, 30 women and children

- Miracle Hill Shepherd's Gate, Greenville, SC, capacity 62 women and children

- Miracle Hill Thrift Operations: six thrift stores in four Upstate counties

Miracle Hill Ministries Executive Leadership

Over the years the following have served in executive leadership positions:

John Bell	Superintendent	1944-1952
George McDowell	Superintendent	(briefly) late 1940's
John Hilley	Superintendent	1953-1954
Waymon Pritchard	Superintendent	1954-1956
Tom Kirk	President	1956-1966
Gerald Lehman	Executive Director	1967-1985
Reid Lehman	President/CEO	1985-Present